ımber.

The Elements of Legal Style

The Elements of Legal Style

SECOND EDITION

Bryan A. Garner

UNIVERSITY PRESS

2002

OXFORD
UNIVERSITY PRESS

Oxford New York
Auckland Bangkok Buenos Aires Cape Town Chennai
Dar es Salaam Delhi Hong Kong Istanbul Karachi Kolkata
Kuala Lumpur Madrid Melbourne Mexico City Mumbai
Nairobi São Paulo Shanghai Singapore Taipei Tokyo Toronto

and associated companies in Berlin

Copyright © 2002 by Bryan A. Garner

Published by Oxford University Press, Inc.
198 Madison Avenue, New York, New York 10016

Oxford is a registered trademark of Oxford University Press

Library of Congress Cataloging-in-Publication Data
Garner, Bryan A.
    The elements of legal style / Bryan A. Garner.--2nd ed.
        p.cm.
    Includes bibliographical references and index.
    ISBN 0-19-514152-8
    1. Legal composition. 2. Law--United States--Language. 3. Law--United
States--Methodology. I. Title.

KF250.G37 2002
808'.06634--dc21   2001055476

Book design and composition by Susan Day

9 8 7 6 5 4 3 2 1

Printed in the United States of America
on acid-free paper

For Caroline

CONTENTS

ACKNOWLEDGMENTS

Many people have helped shape this book—fellow law teachers, participants in my legal seminars, law students, English professors, and lawyers with literary interests. My friends and colleagues have been exceedingly generous.

The first edition benefited from the efforts of many who read and commented on the entire manuscript: Michael Adams, Thomas Cable, Betty S. Flowers, Gary T. Garner, William R. Keffer, James Knox, Roy M. Mersky, Hal R. Ray Jr., Christopher Ricks, Christopher Simoni, Martin Stanford, Pat Sullivan, John W. Velz, and Charles Alan Wright. Many others read and commented on specific chapters: Griffin B. Bell, Beverly Ray Burlingame, Erwin N. Griswold, Roy J. Grogan Jr., John L. Hauer, Douglas Laycock, Sanford Levinson, Kendrick MacDowell, and Thomas M. Reavley.

For the second edition, several of my colleagues at my company, LawProse, Inc., read and commented on the revised manuscript: Tiger Jackson, Jeffrey Newman, Elizabeth Powell, and David W. Schultz. And my favorite copy editor, Karen Magnuson, went through both the manuscript and the proofs with a keen eye.

Tiger Jackson gave up a little chunk of her life to update and supplement the index. And by the way, anyone who wonders about how significantly the book has grown in the second edition should take the time to look over the index.

My editors at Oxford University Press, first Linda Halvorson and more recently Casper Grathwohl, were tremendously helpful at all stages of production. My wife, Teo, and our daughters, Caroline and Alexandra, cheered me along the way. To them is attributable any good humor that shines through, and so much more.

Bryan A. Garner

In 1987, when Oxford University Press asked me to review and comment on its forthcoming book, *A Dictionary of Modern Legal Usage*, by Bryan A. Garner, I accepted immediately. I did not know Bryan Garner. Although he is a graduate of the law school where I teach, the school is large and he had not been in any of my classes. It was the title, rather than the name of the author, that intrigued me. The title is an obvious allusion to H. W. Fowler's great book, *A Dictionary of Modern English Usage*, originally published in 1926 and now in a second edition, edited by Sir Ernest Gowers, published in 1965. To attempt to do for the language of the law what Fowler did for the English language generally would be an immensely valuable contribution. But to do it in a way that would be up to the lofty standard that Fowler set would be a daunting challenge for anyone, and especially for a 28-year-old barely out of law school.

When I read *DMLU*, as it is often referred to, I was surprised and delighted. Garner had met the difficult challenge. His book does not suffer in a comparison with Fowler. Like his great predecessor, Garner is sensible and authoritative, he writes with great clarity, and he is almost always pithy and often witty. His book has had rave reviews all over the world, from publications as scattered as the *Harvard Law Review, The New Zealand Law Journal,* and *The Times Literary Supplement.* It has attracted so large an audience that it is now available in paperback. It is cited respectfully by courts, including the United States Supreme Court.

It is not surprising that a book on legal usage, expertly done, should attract a large audience. The only tool of the lawyer is words. We have no marvelous pills to prescribe for our patients. Whether we are trying a case, writing a brief, drafting a contract, or negotiating with an adversary, words are the only things we have to work with. The great goal in writing and speaking is clarity. Persuasion is important, but we cannot persuade if we are not clear in saying what we want done and why it ought to be done. The rules of usage developed over the centuries are intended to produce clarity. Observance of them lends a professional polish to the product, and this in turn inspires confidence that the writer or speaker is equally professional and equally competent on matters of substance.

I have worked hard over the years to be a good writer. I have studied the great masters on English usage and style. Even so, I have learned much from Garner, so much in fact that I keep one set of his books within arm's reach in my office, a second similarly close in my study at home, and a third in my secretaries' office to guide them.

Now Garner has taken on a new, and even more difficult, challenge. The title of the present book immediately invites comparison with the book known to the world as "Strunk & White." *The Elements of Style,* written originally by William Strunk, Jr., was revised and popularized by E. B. White and is now in a third edition, published in 1979. There is great wisdom to be found in its 85 pages, and many people have become better writers from studying it. Garner has undertaken to deal with style in legal writing in the pattern and form used by Strunk and White. Writing about style is a more difficult challenge than writing about usage because there are rules about usage. Certainly there are gray areas where informed people may differ on what the rule should be, but there are rules and reasons for them. Style, on the other hand, is a much more personal matter. No one would ever confuse the literary style of Benjamin Cardozo with that of Robert Jackson, even though both of them conformed to the rules of usage. Style turns on what you put into your writing. As Garner points out in Rule 7.2, the dissent of the first Justice Harlan in *Plessy v. Ferguson* shows "magnanimity and empathy," while Justice Brown's majority opinion in that notorious case "shows what can happen when you write with your head but not your heart." There often are many ways, all of them correct by the rules of usage, in which to express a particular idea. Making the best choice among the possibilities requires an ear for the language, a good sense of taste and of tactics, and an instinctive feel for what will work best in a particular situation. These choices are more informed, however, if the writer or speaker is aware of the possibilities and sensitive to the considerations that go into the choice. Garner provides sound guidance on these matters of style for the legal writer, just as Strunk and White have done for years to those writing on more general subjects.

I had the privilege of reading *The Elements of Legal Style* in manuscript. I am confident that anyone, no matter how good a writer, will find much that is useful in the book. My only misgiving is that the book may be too interesting. I have found that *DMLU* takes a lot of my time, because when I look up one thing I am irresistibly drawn to reading many other entries on which my eye falls. I have an uneasy feeling that *Elements* is going to provide the same sort of pleasant temptation.

Charles Alan Wright
December 1990

The Elements of Legal Style

ONE

The Letters of the Law

Why should we need a book on the elements of *legal* style? After all—above all—good legal style is good English style. Take the opinions of Justice Oliver Wendell Holmes, Justice Robert H. Jackson, or Judge Learned Hand; the commentary of William Prosser or Fred Rodell; or the advocacy of Clarence Darrow. These lawyers wrote superb prose. If that's your aim as well, then a thorough understanding of Strunk and White's *The Elements of Style* might be all you need.

Since law is a literary profession, lawyers and judges have much to learn from that book, but we also sense that something is lacking. When we come upon rules such as "Do not use dialect unless your ear is good," or "Make sure the reader knows who is speaking," we conclude that the authors of *The Elements of Style* address primarily novelists, not us. We feel uneasy about their rule "Do not explain too much"; for the legal writer, explaining too little all but ensures failure. However much we might like to "Avoid foreign languages," we cannot do without *voir dire, res ipsa loquitur, de minimis,* and dozens of other Latin and French phrases.

Like authors of other general style manuals, Strunk and White don't speak fully to legal writers. True, our goals are often similar to those of other writers, but we face special problems. For example, we constantly struggle to distinguish terms of art from highfalutin jargon, and that from useful professional shorthand. (Avoid foreign languages, yes—but when and how?) We use ordinary English words in extraordinary senses, and extraordinary English words in senses ordinary only to us. We use and cite authorities in peculiar ways.

But the most bedeviling problem we face is of a different order: we have a history of wretched writing, a history that reinforces itself every time we open the lawbooks. It would take hundreds of prolific Holmeses and Prossers and Darrows to counterbalance all the poor models that continually fortify the lawyer's bad habits.

Daily encountering these models, many of us set legal writing apart from other literary endeavors, just as we delude ourselves into believing that good legal reasoning differs from good reasoning in general. We persist in making our profession exclusive, all the while rationalizing our inability to write well by invoking the age-old legal standards. If Strunk and White did not address us directly—to the exclusion of the rest of humanity ("nonlawyers," as we say)—then of what use is their book? Not being lawyers, they did not understand our special circumstances.

In truth, though, our circumstances aren't so very special. Legal writers must recognize what the rest of the literary world already knows: a good style powerfully improves substance. Indeed, it largely *is* substance. Good legal style consists mostly in figuring out the substance precisely and accurately, and then stating it clearly.

Too many of us equate artful writing, or "style," with the warrior's cumbersome headdress, pleasing to the eye but irrelevant (perhaps even a hindrance) to the conquest. Music provides the better analogy. Does anyone fail to recognize that a Beethoven symphony becomes a different piece when played by an ensemble of kazoos instead of a major symphony orchestra? The medium is the music. Why should we find it difficult to accept the parallel truth in writing?

Take two lines from Samuel Taylor Coleridge's "Rime of the Ancient Mariner":

Alone, alone, all, all alone
Alone on a wide, wide sea![1]

We can capture the information contained in these lines by saying, "Alone on the ocean." But we have lost much of the meaning—the voice and the tone and the mood. We have obliterated the special way in which the poet expressed himself. Writers meet constantly with choices in expression. Word choice, sentence structure, sequences of thought—these may all vary while the message remains the same. But each variation gives the reader a different impression. A solid sense of style guides you to the better, more effective choices, which evoke from readers precisely the desired impressions.

What Is Style?

We can hardly improve on Jonathan Swift's formulation of style: "proper words in proper places." That focuses on the right level of detail, but it begs questions of propriety. What are proper words? And how do you know where their proper places are?

In judging words and their placement, remember that the character of the writer determines the character of the prose. Even when the subject is as alien from everyday life as the Rule in Shelley's Case, style reveals self as surely as anything else. What you say and how you say it reflects your mental habits. In trying to write your best, you may strive to proportion one part to another and to the whole, to accent what matters most, to cut out what is useless, and to preserve a uniform tone throughout. But even with these goals in mind, different writers—however skilled—will approach a topic differently, often quite differently.

Style embodies the message, delivers it for circulation. When style suffers—because of poor organization, sloppy paragraphing,

---

1. Part 4, stanza 1 (1798).

clumsy rhythms, thoughtless jangles, or other befogging lapses—
the content also suffers. When the style is good, the content benefits.
Though all lawyers pay lip service to the importance of good
legal writing, not so many appreciate the capacity of style to influence results. Listen to Lord Denning, probably the greatest of
Britain's judicial stylists:

> [Y]ou must cultivate a style which commands attention. No matter
> how sound your reasoning, if it is presented in a dull and turgid set-
> ting, your hearers—or your readers—will turn aside. They will not
> stop to listen. They will flick over the pages. But if it is presented in a
> lively and attractive setting, they will sit up and take notice. They will
> listen as if spellbound. They will read you with engrossment.[2]

So convinced is Lord Denning of the importance of style that he
attributes the British role in winning World War II as much to
Winston Churchill's manner of speaking and writing as to
Churchill's strategy or intelligence.[3]

For the sake of lesser battles, this book sets out to help you develop an effective legal style. As used in these pages, the phrase *legal
style* refers generally to expository prose about legal subjects,
whether in the form of persuasion, narration, description, or
analysis. Most forms of legal writing fall within the scope of this
book: judicial opinions, advocacy, scholarly commentary, opinion
letters, and other writing in and about law. Legal drafting—for instance, of legislation, rules, and contracts—requires separate treatment and has received it in some excellent works.[4]

The chief aim of style is clarity. But achieving clarity is only the

---

2. LORD DENNING, THE FAMILY STORY 216 (1981; repr. 1982).
3. *Id.*
4. *See, e.g.*, BRYAN A. GARNER, GUIDELINES FOR DRAFTING AND EDITING COURT
   RULES (1996); SCOTT J. BURNHAM, THE CONTRACT DRAFTING GUIDEBOOK (1992);
   BARBARA CHILD, DRAFTING LEGAL DOCUMENTS (2d ed. 1992); JANICE C. REDISH,
   HOW TO WRITE REGULATIONS AND OTHER LEGAL DOCUMENTS IN CLEAR ENGLISH
   (1991); REED DICKERSON, THE FUNDAMENTALS OF LEGAL DRAFTING (2d ed. 1986);
   see also BRYAN A. GARNER, LEGAL WRITING IN PLAIN ENGLISH 119 (2001).

first step; much remains—brevity, for example, and accuracy. Variety, elegance, imagination, force, and wit can make your prose convincing as well as clear. Often you must do more than simply communicate; you must persuade.

Don't confuse the negative with the positive virtues of writing: avoiding grammatical and rhetorical mistakes will not make you an exemplary stylist. Despite what some writing texts might have you believe, there are no formulas for a good prose style. Removing passive-voice verbs, keeping sentences short, and using "action" verbs usually improve a piece of writing, but they still may not result in a good style.

Everything hangs on context and purpose. We value simplicity, but writing as simply as possible does not always mean writing simply. Complicated language occasionally proves unavoidable. Take the legislative jungle that is the tax code: "It can never be made simple, but we can try to avoid making it needlessly complex."[5] We can try to say it in plain language.

But what is "plain language"? I define it as the idiomatic and grammatical use of language that most effectively presents ideas to the reader. By that definition, plain language may be, in some sense, unplain. Who would call Kant's categorical imperative plain, despite the seeming simplicity of the words? "Act as if the maxim on which you act were to become, through your will, a universal law." On the other hand, who would volunteer to simplify it?

Still, most of us aren't framing Kantian thoughts. We should stick to a plain approach. Our age prefers it.

Two Rhetorical Traditions

If we look to the history of rhetoric, we find that our Western legacy contains more than plain bequests. From classical Greek and Roman times, two literary traditions have grown alongside

5. Dobson v. Comm'r, 320 U.S. 489, 495 (1943) (per Jackson, J.).

each other. One, a florid oratorical style called Asiatic prose, sports elaborate antitheses, complicated syntax, and correspondences in sense and sound. The other, Attic prose, is refined conversation: concise, restrained, shorn of intricacy. Both styles came naturally to Cicero, one of the great lawyers of antiquity. Immensely articulate, he began his career with a strong Asiatic bent, which he restrained as he matured. Fortunately, he left a record of his thoughts about forensic style. An eloquent lawyer, wrote Cicero, must prove, must please, and must sway or persuade:

> For these three functions of the orator there are three styles, the plain [Attic] style for proof, the middle style for pleasure, the vigorous [Asiatic] style for persuasion. . . . Now the man who controls and combines these three varied styles needs rare judgment and great endowment; for he will decide what is needed at any point, and will be able to speak in any way which the case requires.[6]

Cicero concluded that an eloquent speaker "can discuss trivial matters in a plain style, matters of moderate significance in the tempered style, and weighty affairs in the grand manner."[7]

Perhaps English-speaking lawyers have reached too often for weighty grandeur. We find oratory and brief-writing about slip-and-fall cases that, by implication, would put them on a par with the most important constitutional issues. The style, we might say, does not match the subject matter. Or, as Swift might have put it, improper words have been put in improper places, or improper words in proper places, or proper words in improper places. In that confusion lies the rhetorical origin of legalese, a bastardized Asiatic style.

Whatever claims legalese may have to legal tradition, modern readers—even of lawbooks—prefer the Attic style. We like what is

6. Cicero, *Orator* §§ 69–70, at 357, *in* BRUTUS, ORATOR (H.M. Hubbell trans., 1939; rev. & repr. 1962).
7. *Id.* § 101, at 379.

plain; we grow impatient with what is fancy. Legal readers admire directness and scorn baroque curlicues.

In other periods, Asiatic writers have reached great heights. The Asiatic style may not be to your taste or mine, but it has produced some great literature. One thinks of the prose of John Milton, Samuel Johnson, Edmund Burke, or Thomas De Quincey. A one-sentence extract from *The Rambler* illustrates Johnson's style:

> Among other opposite qualities of the mind which may become dangerous, though in different degrees, I have often had occasion to consider the contrary effects of presumption and despondency; of heady confidence, which promises victory without contest, and heartless pusillanimity, which shrinks back from the thought of great undertakings, confounds difficulty with impossibility, and considers all advancement towards any new attainment as irreversibly prohibited.[8]

Few 20th-century writers—not even Benjamin Cardozo—would choose Johnson's high-flown words. True, Cardozo went as far as to write, "The decree under review protects the petitioner with sedulous forethought against an oppressive inquisition";[9] but Johnson might well have gone further, as by substituting *prepense* for *forethought*.

Cardozo best exemplifies the refined Asiatic style in modern legal writing, as when he described this very style in judicial opinions. He called this style

> the refined or artificial, smelling a little of the lamp. With its merits it has its dangers, for unless well kept in hand, it verges at times upon preciosity and euphuism. Held in due restraint, it lends itself admirably to cases where there is need of delicate precision. I find no better organon where the subject matter of discussion is the construction of a will with all the filigree of tentacles, the shades and

---

8. Samuel Johnson, *The Rambler*, No. 25, 12 June 1750, *in* 1 SAMUEL JOHNSON & PERI-ODICAL LITERATURE: THE RAMBLER 145, 147 (1978).
9. Sinclair Refining Co. v. Jenkins Petroleum Process Co., 289 U.S. 689, 697 (1933).

nuances of differences, the slender and fragile tracery that must be preserved unmutilated and distinct.[10]

More than anything else, Cardozo's Asiatic indulgences differentiate his style from that of Holmes. When commentators contrast Holmes's style with Cardozo's—usually extolling the one and inveighing against the other—what they unwittingly observe is that Holmes inclined toward the Attic, Cardozo toward the Asiatic style.

Conversation vs. Contrivance

Holmes's Attic style moves more swiftly than Cardozo's Asiatic style. Even the long sentence in the following extract reads as if it were recorded conversation, not contrived verbal finery:

> Persecution for the expression of opinions seems to me perfectly logical. If you have no doubt of your premises or your power and want a certain result with all your heart you naturally express your wishes in law and sweep away all opposition. To allow opposition by speech seems to indicate that you think the speech impotent, as when a man says that he has squared the circle, or that you do not care wholeheartedly for the result, or that you doubt either your power or your premises. But when men have realized that time has upset many fighting faiths, they may come to believe even more than they believe the very foundations of their own conduct that the ultimate good desired is better reached by free trade in ideas—that the best test of truth is the power of the thought to get itself accepted in the competition of the market, and that truth is the only ground upon which their wishes safely can be carried out. That, at any rate, is the theory of our Constitution. It is an experiment, as all life is an experiment. Every year, if not every day, we have to wager our salvation upon some prophecy based upon imperfect knowledge.[11]

Even without knowing the Attic and Asiatic styles, jurists have recognized the differences between Holmes's style and Cardozo's.

---

10. Benjamin N. Cardozo, *Law and Literature*, 52 Harv. L. Rev. 472, 481 (1939).
11. Abrams v. United States, 250 U.S. 616, 630 (1919) (Holmes, J., dissenting).

Take three typical statements from legal literature. First: "Holmes could put in a sentence a thought that would take Cardozo a page, and yet Cardozo's graceful, old-fashioned English is a delight to read, and in its own gentle way, it is as unique as Holmes's."[12] Conceding that "Cardozo's style had certain charms," another commentator remarks: "His style, cold and smooth and at times irritatingly precious, was a mere adornment for fairly conventional ideas. In contrast to the spontaneity and fire of Holmes's best pages, those of Cardozo are artificial and lifeless."[13] And this, from one recalling his legal schooling: "[A]nother professor [at Harvard], whom we called 'Bull' Warren . . . , would get absolutely apoplectic in discussing the opinions of Justice Cardozo, whom we students most admired for his lucidity and flowing style. His objections were centered mainly, as we gathered, on Cardozo's style of putting the subject last."[14]

So offensive was Cardozo's Asiatic style to Jerome Frank that he accused Cardozo of retreating from the 20th century and reemerging "disguised as an 18th-century scholar and gentleman."[15] Frank said that Cardozo wrote "of 20th-century America not in the idiom of today but in a style that employed the obsolescent 'King's English' of two hundred years ago." Thus Cardozo's Asiatic habits: "inverted expressions [what Professor Warren detested], negative

12. Ray Henson, *A Study in Style: Mr. Justice Frankfurter*, 6 VILL. L. REV. 377, 378 (1961).
13. David Weissman, *"Supremecourtese": A Note on Legal Style*, 14 LAW. GUILD REV. 138, 139 (1954).
14. Philip Goodheim, *Literary Style and Legal Writing, or, Why Not Throw Some Literary Effort into Preparing Mr. Blackstone's Chowder?*, 37 N.Y. ST. B.J. 529, 529–30 (1965). Note that Cardozo has also been much praised, as by Judge Charles E. Clark, who said that Cardozo's "own standard of literary effort was so high as to make our lesser attempts seem feeble indeed." *State Law in the Federal Courts*, 55 YALE L.J. 267, 268 (1946). And by Justice Frankfurter: "The bar reads [Cardozo's] opinions for pleasure, and even a disappointed litigant must feel, when Judge Cardozo writes, that a cause greater than his private interest prevailed." FELIX FRANKFURTER, LAW AND POLITICS 103, 106 (1939).
15. Jerome Frank, *The Speech of Judges: A Dissenting Opinion*, 29 VA. L. REV. 625, 630 (1943) (published anonymously). For Frank's acknowledgment of authorship of that essay, see Frank, *Some Reflections on Judge Learned Hand*, 24 U. CHI. L. REV. 666, 672 n.18 (1957).

constructions, sinuous turns of phrase, elaborate metaphors."
Frank, a confirmed Atticist (without so phrasing it), preferred the
writings of Thoreau and Justice Holmes, which he said "are full of
native idioms; are made of the American speech of their day,
heightened and polished."[16]

Deciding What's Good

Frank's statements lead us to important questions. What is it that
makes us say, "This is good legal writing"? Why do we decide that a
brief or judicial opinion is well written? What do we value in writing? When we habitually ask these questions, we awaken the critical faculty. We come to recognize that style often differentiates the
workaday from the great judge. To contemplate a contradiction,
imagine if Holmes had been just as brilliant a jurist but devoid of
stylistic genius: would American law have taken quite the same
course?

We remember and reread great opinions largely because they are
well written. Leading cases have likely become so by virtue of
memorable opinions. We may be less interested in the subject matter than in how the judge has dealt with it. By contrast, even the
best material can be spoiled by an inept hand.

"Fine," you may say, "but what do masters like Holmes and Cardozo have to do with me, an unremarkable writer without literary
aspirations?" Analyzing their prose may be no more helpful to you
than showing films of Ben Hogan or Babe Zaharias to a novice
golfer. Perhaps we cannot learn to write greatly—only to avoid
writing poorly.[17] But whatever your individual abilities, the masters provide the best models.

More particularly, the *Attic* masters provide good models. They
suit our time. We can admire an Asiatic writer like Cardozo from

---

16. 29 VA. L. REV. at 629.
17. *See* RICHARD A. POSNER, LAW AND LITERATURE: A MISUNDERSTOOD RELATION 297
(1988).

afar, appreciating his style without trying to imitate it. But those of us less talented than Cardozo will stumble—or plunge—when we try it. (Even he did not always succeed.) Before experimenting with the showier qualities in writing, master the art that conceals art: try to be direct, simple, lucid, and brief.

To be sure, Cardozo's style was sometimes all of those things, especially in factual narrative. Indeed, his statement of the facts in *Palsgraf v. Long Island Railroad*[18] has been hailed as a model of plain language.[19] But his literary flair was not plain, and it sometimes betrayed him when he attempted to elevate the mundane. He once wrote, for example, in an opinion addressing whether a man who paid his employer's debts could take a tax deduction: "Life in all its fullness must supply the answer to the riddle."[20] Did anyone ever write an emptier sentence?[21]

In the judgment of Karl Llewellyn, that great analyst of judicial opinions, it is where Cardozo "is off-base that the creaking ornament and oversubtle phrasing chiefly flourish."[22] How, then, do we find ornaments that don't creak and phrases that have just the right degree of subtlety? For most of us, it's best to be wary of ornament and subtlety. Still, we need not forswear them altogether. How much less engaging, for example, Llewellyn's own writing would have been without them![23]

In every context, we must weigh what is appropriate. We need not—should not—suppress all the literary devices at hand. Even the Attic style uses them. Nor should we seek one style as the ideal for all legal writing, any more than we should force on society an

---

18. 248 N.Y. 339, 340–41, 162 N.E. 99, 99 (1928).
19. *See* RICHARD C. WYDICK, PLAIN ENGLISH FOR LAWYERS 5–6 (4th ed. 1998).
20. Welch v. Helvering, 290 U.S. 111, 115 (1933).
21. *See* Erwin N. Griswold, *Foreword: The Supreme Court 1959 Term*, 74 HARV. L. REV. 81, 90 (1960).
22. KARL LLEWELLYN, THE COMMON LAW TRADITION: DECIDING APPEALS 37 n.29 (1960).
23. For examples, see 6.3, 6.10, 6.16, 6.19, 6.21, 6.22, 6.23.

absolute dress code. A formal dinner may require evening clothes, but they would be out of place on the beach. The law has its beaches as well as its stately ceremonies, and much in between. We should not try to make it always solemn.

Fluffy Speech Not Required

Holmes once found himself the object of censure by Chief Justice Charles Evans Hughes for writing that amplifications in a statute would "stop rat holes" in it. Hughes felt that the phrase was too racy. Holmes recalled his answer: "I said our reports were dull because we had the notion that judicial dignity required solemn fluffy speech, as, when I grew up, everybody wore black frock coats and black cravats."[24] That "fluffy speech" is the source to this day of the monotone we hear upon opening virtually any volume of American judicial opinions.

We are right to judge what is good and bad in writing, what is effective and ineffective. Ultimately, everything is good that is "conceived with honesty and executed with communicative ardor."[25] Or, as Voltaire said, "Every style is good save that which bores."[26]

This, then, is a handbook about how not to bore your readers. Legal writing shouldn't be lethal reading. Your readers are the ones, finally, who matter: you have invited them to attend to your words, you seek their precious time, and you may even expect to be paid for your efforts. Courtesy requires that you show your readers some grace and consideration.

Don't just expect their interest. Arouse it. That dictum (if only

---

24. 2 HOLMES–POLLOCK LETTERS 132 (M. Howe ed., 1941) (adding, in reference to the latter phrase, "I didn't say that to them.").
25. ROBERT LOUIS STEVENSON, LEARNING TO WRITE 30 (1888; repr. 1920).
26. "[T]outs les genres sont bons, hors le genre ennuyeux." Voltaire, Preface to *L'Enfant Prodigue, in* 3 OEUVRES COMPLÈTES DE VOLTAIRE 442, 445 (1877) (*genre* meaning "le style de l'auteur" [Littré]).

we could make it a mandate!) runs counter to everything that legal writing is about. Judges are paid to evaluate lawyers' writing, whether in a brief or in a simple court paper. To thwart their opponents' work, lawyers must read and understand it, and (of course) must analyze judicial opinions. There can be no doubt: we're not in the business of pleasure reading.

Then why make someone else's task more enjoyable by increasing your own effort? The answer lies in success, in results: Holmes did it; Cardozo did it; Jackson and Hand did it; so did Prosser and Rodell and Darrow. If, as an advocate, you do it, you may make your opponent's reading easier; but you also upset your opponent because you reduce the judge's work and increase your likelihood of winning. If you do it as a judge, you add distinction to the judiciary as well as to your opinions, which will fare better in the esteem of your fellow lawyers; you're stating the law better for the present and the future.

Whenever you do it, in whatever capacity, you add luster to the letters of the law.

TWO

Fundamental Rules of Usage

PUNCTUATION

> [M]en's lives may depend upon a comma....
> *Johnson, J.*[1]

2.1 Always use the serial comma.

The serial comma separates items, including the last from the next to last, in a list of more than two. It makes the phrasing parallel:

the defendants, the third-party defendants, and the counterdefendants.

The question whether to include the final comma in an enumerated series has sparked many arguments in law offices and judges' chambers. The reason for preferring the final comma is that omitting it may cause ambiguities, while including it never will. For example, confusion arises when one of the final members contains two elements:

The investor asked for separate reports on the performance of her investments in real estate, commodities, coins and stocks and bonds.

---

1. United States v. Palmer, 16 U.S. (3 Wheat.) 610, 636 (1818) (dissenting). For an English example of life depending on a comma, see Rex v. Casement, [1917] 1 K.B. 98 (1916).

The serial comma clears up the clouded relationship of *coins, stocks,* and *bonds.* A comma after *coins* gives one meaning. The investor wants four reports, dealing with

real estate, commodities, coins, and stocks and bonds.

Punctuating the sentence differently shows another kind of association. The investor may want the reports grouped differently:

real estate, commodities, coins, stocks, and bonds (five reports)

real estate, commodities, coins and stocks, and bonds (four reports)

real estate; commodities; and coins, stocks, and bonds (three reports).

There is only one conventional exception to the serial-comma rule. Omit the comma before an ampersand:

Staveley, MacCormick & Tuppington, P.C.

Monse, Lovell & Co.

The serial comma will often help you avoid ambiguity. So make a habit of using it consistently, regardless of whether ambiguity threatens to invade your sentence.

2.2   Set off a dependent introductory phrase with a comma.

Generally, you should set off a phrase that comes before the main clause. Unless an introductory phrase is essential to the meaning of the sentence, you should punctuate it with a comma.

Not this:	*But this:*
In waiving sovereign immunity the legislature must express a clear intention to waive immunity against claims of a particular kind.	In waiving sovereign immunity, the legislature must express a clear intention to waive immunity against claims of a particular kind.

An exception: when the sentence or the introductory phrase

consists of one or two words—and your ear so counsels—you may omit the comma. On this principle, many expressions of time are not set off.

By October the debt had climbed to more than $10,000.

But: By October 2001, the debt had climbed to more than $10,000.

In 1989 the Litigation Section was the ABA's second largest.

But: During most of the late 1980s, the Litigation Section was the ABA's second largest.

2.3 Put a comma between two adjectives that modify a noun similarly.

Paired adjectives may independently modify a noun, so that you could switch their order without affecting the meaning. To state the relationship negatively, the first adjective in the pair neither depends on nor modifies the second adjective, as here:

an ambitious, entrepreneurial woman

a reserved, cautious person

a simplistic, fallacious conclusion

But when adjectives qualify the noun in different ways, or when one adjective qualifies another, don't use a comma:

a Scottish legal theorist

a distinguished foreign journalist

a small white rabbit

Here's a simple test to use if you're ever in doubt about the need for a comma to separate adjectives. As you read the adjectives, silently put *and* between them. If the *and* makes perfectly good sense (*a reserved and cautious person*), then place a comma after the first adjective. If the *and* seems awkward, forced, or otherwise inappropriate (*a small and white rabbit*), omit the comma.

2.4   Put a comma before the second clause in a compound sentence.

The comma separates independent clauses joined by coordinating conjunctions: *and*, *but*, *or*, *nor*, and *for*.

> The United States is a common-law country, and its judges are common-law judges.[2]

> We can probe only so far into people's motives, and sometimes a little restraint is in order.

> The judge denied the motion to dismiss the charges, but she lowered the defendant's bail.

The exception occurs when compact main clauses have the same subject. Avoid the comma if (1) the subject is not expressed in the second clause, and (2) the clauses aren't particularly long:

> He did it and never regretted it.

> The good brief should address all the issues and should analyze them intelligently.

> The judge was perturbed by the defendant's outbursts but maintained order.

> The brief was short and the judge read it quickly.

2.5   Avoid using a comma to combine two sentences into one.

Don't splice sentences together with a mere comma. If you fail to include a coordinating conjunction (such as *and* or *but*) to hold the independent clauses together, you create what grammarians call a run-on sentence or comma splice. For example:

> The rule fastens liability on the employer where his employee is negligent, otherwise there is no liability.

---

2. ERWIN N. GRISWOLD, LAW AND LAWYERS IN THE UNITED STATES 61 (1964).

You might correct this sentence in either of two ways. One is to insert a semicolon after *negligent* (and put a comma after *otherwise*):

> The rule fastens liability on the employer where his employee is negligent; otherwise, there is no liability.

Another solution is to use a period after *negligent* and then to begin a new sentence:

> The rule fastens liability on the employer where his employee is negligent. Otherwise, there is no liability.

Take another run-on:

> The commission prescribes two levels of qualification, one is for principals and the other for registered representatives.

To fashion a single acceptable sentence, you have several easy solutions. First, you might replace the comma with a semicolon and retain the rest of the sentence as written:

> The commission prescribes two levels of qualification; one is for principals and the other for registered representatives.

Second, if you wish to emphasize how the second half of the sentence specifies the generalization of the first half—if you want to underscore for the reader how one half balances the other—then use a colon:

> The commission prescribes two levels of qualification: one is for principals and the other is for registered representatives.

Finally, if you wish to underscore the separateness of the two *levels of qualification,* delete the word *and* and insert a semicolon:

> The commission prescribes two levels of qualification: one is for principals; the other is for registered representatives.

Of course, several other sound revisions are possible, including this concise one:

The commission prescribes two levels of qualification: one for principals and one for registered representatives.

2.6 Form singular possessives by adding *'s* to the singular form of the noun.

The rule holds true regardless of how the word ends: thus, *witness's, Jones's, Congress's,* and *testatrix's.* There are five exceptions. First, the word *its* is possessive, *it's* being the contraction for *it is.* Second, *yours, hers,* and *theirs,* which are absolute possessives, take no apostrophe. Third, biblical and classical names that end with a *-zes* or *-eez* sound take only the apostrophe:

Jesus' teachings
Moses' lifetime
Aristophanes' plays
Socrates' arguments

If the possessive forms seem awkward to you, rephrase: *the laws of Moses* instead of *Moses' laws, the action of Congress* or *the congressional action* instead of *Congress's action.* Fourth, if a corporate or similar name is formed from a plural word, it takes only the apostrophe:

General Motors' board of directors
Scribes' history (referring to the legal organization known as
    Scribes)
Swatzell Investors' advice on stocks

Finally, a sibilant possessive before *sake* takes merely an apostrophe, without an additional *-s*—hence *for goodness' sake* and *for conscience' sake.*

2.7 Form a plural possessive by adding an apostrophe to the plural form of the noun: *-s'.*

Hence, *the Atwoods', the Burnses', the Joneses', bosses', octopuses', witnesses'.* Some writers err, though probably not as speakers, by merging this rule with that for making singular nouns possessive:

> John Rogers, the perkmeister of the Reagan years, recalled the time
> an official demanded an office in the residential quarters, near the
> *Reagans's* [read *Reagans'*] bedroom.[3]

An exception to the rule: when the plural form does not end in *-s*,
simply add *-'s* (*women's, children's*).

2.8 Use a semicolon to separate sentence parts calling for a stronger break than a comma.

The semicolon is among the least used punctuation marks today,
perhaps because of a growing uncertainty about its proper uses.
There are three. First, the semicolon may join statements too
closely related to be split into two sentences by a period but not related closely enough for a comma to suffice:

> The war had been not merely a profoundly unsettling experience in
> itself; it had also marked for America the beginning of unaccus-
> tomed and vexing entanglements in international affairs.[4]

> The statutes . . . must be viewed against the background of the earlier
> rules that husband and wife are one, and that one the husband; and
> that as the husband took the wife's chattels he was liable for her
> debts.[5]

Second, the semicolon may separate enumerated items that
themselves contain commas, the purpose being to avoid ambiguity
that would otherwise result from using commas in two different
ways:

> The company has offices in Bartlesville, Oklahoma; Theills, New
> York; and Greenville, North Carolina.

---

3. *Washington Talk: The White House*, N.Y. TIMES, 31 Mar. 1989, at A11.
4. ROBERT G. MCCLOSKEY, THE MODERN SUPREME COURT 6 (1972).
5. Hoeper v. Tax Comm'n of Wis., 284 U.S. 206, 219 (1931) (Holmes, J., dissenting).

[P]ermit me to check off a few words as symbols of the various components of the thesis I have been attempting to expound: seeds, growth, inner resources; freedom, curiosity, imagination, creative powers, happiness, and fulfillment; intellectual discipline, the power to write and to speak persuasively and with lucidity; devotion to ideas and moral principles, a warm sympathy and a merciful and understanding heart; courage, integrity, steadfastness; spiritual strength and power.[6]

Finally, the semicolon usefully separates items listed after a colon, as here:

The board of regents gave three reasons for rejecting the committee's report: (1) the report insufficiently addressed the factual allegations that the president had violated faculty members' academic freedom; (2) it did not name any sources for the information on which it relied; and (3) it drew conclusions that the board of regents was unprepared to accept.

That case was followed by numerous others, e.g.: that one person could not be given twice or 10 times the voting power of another person in a statewide election merely because he lived in a rural area or in the smallest rural county; that the principle of equality applied to both Houses of a bicameral legislature; that political parties receive protection under the Equal Protection Clause just as voters do.[7]

Always put semicolons outside quotation marks or parentheses:

"I dislike . . . ," [Montaigne] said, "unpunishable thoughts"; and he admonished, "Let us not be ashamed to say what we are not ashamed to think."[8]

---

6. Harold R. Medina, *The Liberal Arts and the Professions, in* THE ANATOMY OF FREEDOM 35, 47 (C. Waller Barrett ed., 1959).
7. Oregon v. Mitchell, 400 U.S. 112, 136–37 (1970) (Douglas, J., dissenting in part and concurring in part) (footnotes omitted).
8. JEROME FRANK, COURTS ON TRIAL 158–59 (1949; repr. 1950).

2.9   Set off incidental comments with paired marks of punctuation.

For this purpose, use commas, parentheses, or dashes. When interpolating incidental thoughts—a mannerism to keep in check—you have a choice. As in the previous sentence, you may use long dashes, also called em dashes. Or you might write:

> When interpolating incidental thoughts (a mannerism to keep in check), you have a choice.

Yet again, if you prefer, you might write:

> When interpolating incidental thoughts, a mannerism to keep in check, you have a choice.

Of these three marks—dashes, commas, parentheses—the dashes provide the greatest break in the sentence and therefore the strongest emphasis:

> We are proud—rightly—that our system affords these rights; and we regard them—wrongly—as naturally part of that system, ancient and honored axioms.[9]

To reduce emphasis conveyed by dashes, use commas:

> We are proud, rightly, that our system affords these rights; and we regard them, wrongly, as naturally part of that system, ancient and honored axioms.

To diminish the emphasis still further, use parentheses:

> We are proud (rightly) that our system affords these rights; and we regard them (wrongly) as naturally part of that system, ancient and honored axioms.

To give the least emphasis, put the adverbs in their customary syntactic position, closer to the verb:

9. CHARLES REMBAR, THE LAW OF THE LAND 376 (1980).

We are rightly proud that our system affords these rights; and we wrongly regard them as naturally part of that system, ancient and honored axioms.

Whatever your choice of internal punctuation, refrain from festooning a single sentence with commas, parentheses, and dashes. All punctuation, even underlining, slows the reader, as this extreme example shows:

> For the interpolation of incidental thoughts—a mannerism that should <u>not</u>, for the sake of your reader (always first and foremost), be overindulged—you have a choice.

For more on underlining as opposed to italics, see 4.3.

2.10 Hyphenate phrasal adjectives.

Readers shouldn't have to hesitate in telling adjectives from nouns. Yet they must often do just that when the writer fails to show that a phrase that looks like a noun is actually functioning as an adjective. For example, when we first reach, in midsentence, the phrase

> common law mirror image rule

we're likely to see *common law* as the noun, unsuspecting that we'll soon find our true noun in *rule*. The writer lessens our work as readers by forestalling our missteps:

> common-law mirror-image rule.

The general principle is that a phrase, when functioning as an adjective (or compound modifier) before a noun, should be hyphenated. (The only common exception occurs with adverbs ending in -*ly*, such as *widely held opinion*.) The principle applies to countless legal phrases:

> child-support payments
> civil-rights case (*but* proponent of civil rights)
> common-law privilege (*but* the common law, at common law [see
>   p. 107])

good-faith exception
long-latency occupational-disease cases
take-nothing judgment
third-degree assault

Who doesn't hesitate in reading the following sentence?

The benefit of insurance and waiver of subrogation clauses in the affreightment contracts are invalid because they conflict with the
plaintiff's marine cargo insurance policy.

Assuming the need to stick to this basic sentence structure, you
might punctuate that sentence as follows:

The benefit-of-insurance and waiver-of-subrogation clauses in the
affreightment contracts are invalid because they conflict with the
plaintiff's marine-cargo insurance policy.

But snakelike compounds often signal the need to recast the
sentence:

Not this:

The breach-of-contract-claim-
waiver provision was void as
being against public policy.

The law-of-the-case-doctrine dispute might have been settled differently under late-20th-century
jurisprudence.

But this:

The provision waiving claims for
breach of contract was void as
being against public policy.

The dispute over law of the case
might have been settled differently a quarter century ago.

Writers sometimes use overlong phrasal adjectives to achieve a
humorously dismissive tone:

Of these two major means of effective attack on the Court plan, the
don't-touch-the-Court-it's-sacred stuff, while spread across the
country by press, radio, and club-car conversation, was all focused on
the Senate committee-room where heated hearings were under way.[10]

---

10. FRED RODELL, NINE MEN 247 (1955).

2.11 Otherwise, be stingy with hyphens.

Phrasal adjectives aside, the American branch of the English language has become more and more inhospitable to hyphens. Professional writers and editors today prefer that prefixes and their bases be written as solids 99% of the time—that is, as *un*hyphenated single words, whatever the word class of the base may be (adjective, noun, adverb, or verb). Generally, solidify each of the following prefixes when adding it to a base:

a__	mis__
an__	mono__
ante__	multi__
anti__	neo__
auto__	non__
bi__	out__
bio__	over__
co__	pan__
counter__	poly__
de__	post__
di__	pre__
dis__	pro__
extra__	proto__
fore__	pseudo__
hyper__	re__
il__	semi__
im__	sub__
in__	super__
infra__	supra__
inter__	sur__
intra__	trans__
macro__	tri__
mal__	ultra__
meta__	un__
micro__	under__
mid__	uni__
mini__	

Hence, *antiestablishment, antipoverty, cocounsel, coworker, minitrial, noncompetition, nonpayment, postjudgment, preemption, pretrial, superlegislature, unalterable, underestimate.*

For the remaining 1% of the time, use a hyphen to join a prefix to its base when (1) omitting the hyphen would baffle the reader or cause a genuine misreading if the word were spelled as a solid (*hyper-illegible, pre-judicial* [as against *prejudicial*], *re-sign* [as against *resign*]); (2) omitting the hyphen produces a visual monstrosity (*anti-injunction, multi-institutional*); or (3) the base is a proper noun (*intra-African, pro-Philadelphia, anti-Waldheim*).

Yet some prefixes do require hyphens. *Quasi,* for instance, always takes a hyphen when it appears in a compound adjective (*quasi-contractual, quasi-judicial, quasi-public*) and usually also when the compound is a noun (*quasi-deposit, quasi-rent, quasi-usufruct*). *Self-,* when joined to any word (whether adjective or noun), takes a hyphen most of the time (*self-abnegation, self-assured, self-defense*). The exceptions occur when *self* is added to a suffix (*selfdom, selfless, selfness, selfward*) or when the word happens to be *selfsame.*

In American English, noun-plus-noun compounds generally take hyphens in the same circumstances as those of prefix-plus-base compounds. For example, compare three words in American English—*lawbreaker, law-hand,* and *law stationer*—with their counterparts in British English—*law-breaker, law-hand, law-stationer.* Compound words that are old, rare, or regional are likely to retain their hyphens when brought into American English, as are compounds that are awkward without hyphens. But the most common compounds usually lose their hyphens and stand either open or closed. Take, for example, the word *law* coupled with various bases, here in American-English form:

lawbook
lawbreaker
law clerk

law court
lawgiver
law-hand
law lord
lawmaker
lawsuit
law-worthy

Only two of these ten words retain the hyphen: one probably because it is a British historical term rarely used (*law-hand*), the other because of the monstrous look of *-ww-* if the word were written as a solid and the semantic confusion that would occur if it were written as separate words (*law worthy*).

When newly coined, a noun-plus-noun compound is usually hyphenated (*court-room, bench-warrant*). Through repeated use and the passage of time, the hyphen disappears when the compound takes on a clear and familiar meaning, either as a solid or as a separate (*courtroom, bench warrant*). The tendency to solidify also affects many other types of compounds, such as *setoff* and *comeuppance*.

As several students of the language have remarked, it's hard to stay sane if you think long and hard about the logic of hyphens. To save time in writing and editing, make a list of the preferred spellings of words that repeatedly trouble you and keep it handy. Enter them into your computer's spell-checker dictionary if they come up as errors.

2.12 Slash out virgules (/).

Call it a solidus or a slash, if you like, but a virgule by any other name looks just as bad: *and/or, him/her, s/he, Times/Gertz line of cases.* The first three items in that list are abominations to be avoided on other grounds (see pp. 103, 207); the fourth should be written *Times–Gertz line of cases.* The rule says it all.

WORD CHOICE

> The search is for the just word, the happy phrase,
> that will give expression to the thought . . . .
> *Benjamin Cardozo*[11]

Stylists draw upon an ample vocabulary, but without ostentation. They show sensitivity to the tonal grading of words, to the nuances that differentiate near-synonyms, to the unexplainable sense that distinguishes the right word from the almost-right word. Mark Twain compared that distinction to the difference between lightning and the lightning bug. Stylists understand the truth of his gentle hyperbole.

Wording your thoughts is largely a personal matter. Yet certain broad principles—Attic principles—generally hold true in English prose.

Prefer the familiar word to the far-fetched.
Prefer the concrete word to the abstract.
Prefer the single word to the circumlocution.
Prefer the short word to the long.
Prefer the Saxon word to the Romance.[12]

"These rules are given roughly in order of merit," the Fowlers wrote when formulating them, adding that "the last is also the least."[13] Forcefulness explains these rules: how much more force the word *home* carries than *residence*, or *residence* than *habitation*, or *habitation* than *commorancy*. "His brother died" has an immediacy that "His male sibling expired" does not.

Make these rules your own. They'll be helpful as we consider several types of words in legal prose: fancy words, vague words, vogue words, euphemisms, timid phrases, empty dogmatisms, and neologisms.

---

11. THE GROWTH OF THE LAW 89 (1924; repr. 1966).
12. H.W. FOWLER & F.G. FOWLER, THE KING'S ENGLISH 11 (3d ed. 1930).
13. *Id.*

2.13 Strike out and replace fancy words.

In legal writing as in all writing, the object is to communicate effectively. Yet we occasionally encounter writers who seek to demonstrate their own brilliance with an obscure vocabulary. As Jerome Frank put it, "Too many writers identify profundity with obscurity."[14] Profound or obscure? You be the judge:

> [A]ppellants' adhibition of mortality tables and their presentation and argument . . . were predicated . . . on the metachronism that Sally was born before the accident which took her life in 1970 . . . .[15]

One federal appellate judge habitually uses the following words (and many others like them) in his opinions: *decurtate, encincture, eschatocol, furculum, hypoplasia, imbrication, imprecation, inconcinnate, internuncio, neoteric, ossature, perficient, perfrication, perlustration, perscrutation, postcibal, prescind, pruritis, repastinate, resupination, struthious, vaticinate,* and *zoetic.* (In none of the cases did these words appear as a result of the facts at issue.) In an age when many of our judicial opinions lack originality and freshness, this use of the English vocabulary is peculiarly striking. But it strikes us negatively in almost every instance because the writer has strained to find the unfamiliar word when the ordinary one comes immediately to mind. Why *perficient* instead of *efficient,* or *perscrutation* instead of *scrutiny*?

We shouldn't stifle a liberal use of the English vocabulary. Legal literature would be the poorer, for example, if Lord Radcliffe had not reached to define *reasonable man* as the "anthropomorphic conception of justice."[16] But if you use a big word, assure yourself that you have done it because no other term will serve better in context—not because you want to teach your readers a new word. Otherwise, you may find yourself being congratulated for a "'tri-

---

14. COURTS ON TRIAL 416 (1949; repr. 1950).
15. Hines v. Sweet, 567 S.W.2d 435, 438 (Mo. Ct. App. 1978).
16. Davis Contractors Ltd. v. Fareham U.D.C. [1956] A.C. 696, 728–29.

umph of obfuscation, full of big words . . .—all whiz and pizzazz
and canal water.'"[17]

2.14 Challenge vague words.

Vague words abound in law. Reserve them for those contexts where
you truly need them. Think of *fine, bad, good, nice, important,
major, meaningful, significant, interesting.* Many vague words are
nouns, such as *aspect, phase, process, theme,* or those ending in -*tion*
(e.g., *actualization, consideration* [as in *practical considerations*],
manifestation, motivation). The reader comes upon these fuzzy
words and gets a fuzzy impression.

For example, what does the writer mean by this:

> One aspect of the conditions necessary to the actualization of the
> rule of law is the process of creating meaningful access to justice.

Does this mean that the rule of law means little if people can't have
their day in court? It's hard to know, given the airiness of the original. The phrasing, as well as the writer's thinking, needs sharpening.

In certain phrases, such as *bad law* (one that is not sustainable),
bad may actually mean something. But to say of a judicial opinion
that it is a bad precedent does not explain whether you think that
the reasoning is poor, that the judges have disregarded earlier law,
or that the decision promotes degenerate social policy. To say *bad
precedent* is merely to growl. Instead, explain in a simple phrase or
clause what is bad about the precedent, without using the word
bad. Say that it is "poorly reasoned because it ignores the difference
between legal and illegal aliens," if that is your point.

In short, vague words tend to make sentences ineffective. Use
concrete terms, and your readers will have a clearer idea of your
meaning.

---

17. Berg v. Printers' Ink Publ'g Co., 54 F. Supp. 795, 804 (S.D.N.Y. 1943) (quoting a
statement alleged to be libelous).

2.15 Shun vogue words.

Whenever you write a word or phrase that is on the tip of everyone's tongue, strike it out. Vogue words cheapen prose, partly because their fashionableness wears down their meaning to the blandest generality, and partly because they make you sound like an unthinking writer of ready-made phrases. You might easily add to the following list of vogue words and phrases:

> bottom line
> constructive (criticism, engagement, etc.)
> cost-effective, cost-efficient
> cutting edge (or leading edge)
> definitely
> dialogue (noun or verb)
> dimension
> environment (e.g., work environment)
> escalate (= intensify)
> eventuate
> exposure (= liability)
> framework
> hopefully
> impact (as verb)
> input
> interface (except in computer contexts)
> lifestyle
> matrix (except in computer contexts)
> meaningful
> need-to-know basis, on a
> ongoing
> operational
> -oriented (or, worse, "-orientated")
> overall
> overly
> parameters (except in computer contexts)
> point in time
> proactive

to process (a claim, dispute, etc.)
realistic
state-of-the-art
synergy
viability
wait-and-see attitude
-wise (liability-wise, crime-wise)
worst-case scenario

Lawyers use all these phrases, but they also have their own jargonistic vogue words: *three-tiered analysis, balancing test, cost-benefit analysis*, and *two-pronged test*. Have done with them all.

2.16 Eschew euphemisms.

By indirection, euphemisms try to soften what is thought to be disagreeable. Many of them are circumlocutions for death, sex, illness, or bodily functions. We euphemize if we say not that someone is *drunk*, but *inebriated* or *intoxicated*; not that someone is a *drug addict*, but (much more vaguely) is *impaired*; not that someone has *died*, but *passed away*; not that someone is *mentally retarded*, but *exceptional* or *special*. In some contexts, to be sure, you might prefer to euphemize—not least in talking to the widow at the funeral of an impaired acquaintance who was inebriated when he passed away.

But attention-getting euphemisms often gain unwanted attention precisely because they obscure what they are supposed to express. Generally, prefer the direct to the indirect. Avoid novel euphemisms: why becloud the point by saying *sexually ambidextrous* (a special talent?) when *bisexual*, a well-understood word, says what you mean? Readers might infer that the only reason for not using the more familiar word is that you do not want to be fully understood. In the end, then, "Euphemism is more demoralizing than coarseness."[18]

---

18. H.W. FOWLER, A DICTIONARY OF MODERN ENGLISH USAGE 152 (1926).

Many legal euphemisms originated in a Victorian sensibility. Our digests of the law, for example, include sections under the phrase *disorderly houses* because writers consider *whorehouses* or *brothels* or *bordellos* too indelicate. (The nonlegal euphemism is *house of ill fame* or *repute.*) Despite its appearance, *criminal conversation* is not a legal doctrine that runs afoul of the First Amendment; the phrase refers to adulterous sex (which, of course, inevitably interferes with *conjugal felicity*). Only recently have we sloughed off the overzealous euphemizing about homosexuality, known formerly as *the abominable and detestable crime against nature.*

Although some euphemisms, like that last one, are terribly slanted, others result from an understandable desire to sound objective, by avoiding biased words of the past. *Extramarital*, for example, strikes us as more neutral than *adulterous* (as used in the previous paragraph). And many legal writers are now inclined to use *nonmarital children* or *children out of wedlock* instead of *illegitimate children* or, worse yet, *bastards*. Why indeed scar the innocent children with ugly epithets?

But we can carry unjudging blandness too far, to the point of doublespeak, especially in political and military language. *Undocumented worker* is needlessly obscure for *illegal alien*, a descriptive phrase that some consider emotionally charged. Even more obscure are *armed reconnaissance* (bombing), *preventive detention* (imprisonment without an adjudication of guilt), *bureaucratic error* (an executive's blunder), *revenue enhancement* (tax increase), *milieu therapy* (confinement in a mental hospital), *permanent layoff* (you're fired), and *headcount adjustment* (you're fired again).

Generally, a stylist wants the meaning to be easily grasped, even if a few readers may disagree or disapprove. But if plain talk is apt to provoke unnecessary controversy—if talk about *illegitimate children* or *illegal aliens* might divert attention from your point by offending people—then use an established euphemism.

2.17 Toss out timid phrases.

Justice Felix Frankfurter once confessed: "I seemingly cannot write a paragraph without . . . the dull qualifications and circumlocutions that sink any literary barque or even freighter, the lifeless tags and rags that preclude grace and stifle spontaneity."[19] Lawyers are notorious for qualifying every statement they make with weasel words. When they do—by using an unnecessary conditional phrase (*I would contend*) or by saying

it seems

it would appear that

it might be said that

at least as far as X is concerned

it is respectfully suggested that—

they come off as timid and doubtful. Better to state matters confidently and straightforwardly. If you need to convey that what you are saying is only an opinion, do it in some way other than by obscuring whose opinion it is, who's speaking, or under what circumstances the words have effect.

2.18 Discard empty dogmatisms.

Although lawyers often overqualify and sound timid, they also have a penchant for dogmatic words and phrases. This despite the well-known dictum that words such as *obviously, clearly,* and *undoubtedly* are always suspect. Rarely does such a word appear nowadays without blatant hyperbole. Don't use dogmatic words unless even your most ardent opponent would have to concede the truth of what you say. If you use *incontestably* to preface a conclusion about a contested issue, you weaken your argument.

---

19. FELIX FRANKFURTER, LAW AND POLITICS 103, 104 (1939).

Consider these two examples, from briefs submitted to the Supreme Court of the United States:

> While it is undoubtedly true that commerce between the states is much greater now than 200 years ago, this expansion does not change congressional powers. So this is an extremely easy case.
>
> It is clear that the Recruiting Rule clearly applies only to commercial speech. And, most obviously, recruiting by a private school involves commercial transactions.

If these cases are so easy and obvious, why are they before the Supreme Court?

Some depreciative words are likewise objectionably dogmatic. Be careful with such increasingly popular words as *mere, merely, simply,* and *utterly.* The word *simply* now teems in the opinions of the United States Supreme Court, though only a few years ago its use was infrequent.[20] We all know that the Supreme Court decides some of the knottiest issues facing our nation; dogmatic words of this kind simply don't help solve complex legal problems.

Remember: in English, ironically, the phrase *far more* suggests something less than the word *more.* It suggests that you're puffing.

2.19 Be cautious about using neologisms.

American lawyers have often faced the difficulty of calling on a word not to be found in available dictionaries. It's an odd problem. Take, for example, the useful word *conclusory,* much vilified in the late 20th century by a few federal judges who sought its ouster from the legal lexicon. Why? Because it was nowhere in their dictionaries in the sense that lawyers commonly give it—that is, "expressing a factual inference without expressing the specific facts that give rise to the inference." To say "He is a crook" is conclusory in the absence of supporting evidence.

---

20. Stephen R. Barnett, *Simply Put at the Court,* Nat'l L.J., 15 May 1989, at 13.

The chief problem was with the dictionaries' not being up to date.[21] To a great degree the problem has been remedied. The most recent edition of *Black's Law Dictionary*[22] contains some 5,000 new terms, and the major dictionary publishers have added legal editors to their staffs of lexicographers. On the whole, the coverage of legal language in modern dictionaries is noticeably better today than it was 20 years ago. But new words and phrases are continually invented, faster than dictionaries can include them.

Words get invented for a variety of reasons: (1) to denote a technological innovation (*Internet, website, e-filing*); (2) to denote a new idea (*Critical Race Theory, cybersquatting, racial profiling*); (3) to form an adjective to correspond to an existing noun (*alegal, certworthy, litigational, pretextual, restitutionary*); (4) to form a noun corresponding to a verb (*quashal*) or a verb corresponding to a noun (*Mirandize*); or (5) to form an agent noun (*asylee, condemnee, conveyee, fraudfeasor*). Some of these are necessary.

Some aren't necessary. And in the process of linguistic natural selection, many if not most will be discarded—or will live a brief life at the fringes of the language. Others will thrive. Winnowing the one type from the other isn't always easy. But here's a test for achieving some balance. On the one hand, try your best to work within the existing resources of the English language. On the other hand, recognize that if a new word or phrase carries a fresh meaning and provides a genuine shortcut to communication, we should welcome it as a useful addition to the language.

2.20 Tune the levels of usage with a fine ear.

The language of legal prose is a mixture of legal jargon, formal and general English, and an occasional touch of slang. Sometimes the

---

21. *See* Bryan A. Garner, *The Missing Common-Law Words, in* THE STATE OF THE LANGUAGE 235, 239–40 (Christopher Ricks & Leonard Michaels eds., 1990) (noting the history and widespread prevalence of *conclusory* and other words).
22. BLACK'S LAW DICTIONARY (7th ed. 1999).

legal writer wants a formal, bookish tone, at other times a relaxed, earthy colloquiality. Legal writers are usually free to choose the level of usage that best suits their purposes. The three passages that follow illustrate acceptable levels of usage in modern legal writing. In reading each passage, notice how the choice of words affects your reaction.

1. The law may lay down that in order to effect a particular result the will must be expressed in a formal way and that, if the precise form is not carried out, the juristic act will have no effect. The required form may be [a] signed writing attested by two witnesses. A transfer of res mancipi in Roman law required the oral repetition by the parties of set words and the carrying out of certain gestures.

   In other cases the law cares not how the will be expressed, so long as its expression is clear and unambiguous. A nod in an auction room may be accepted by the hammer of the auctioneer . . . . [T]he form of a will is strictly laid down in order that clear evidence of the testator's wishes may be available, and to make forgery more difficult.[23]

2. Our lawyers and citizens recognize a difference between the question what the law is and the question whether judges or any other official or citizen should enforce or obey the law. They regard these as separate questions, not only when they have in mind foreign, wicked legal systems in the various ways we just noticed, but even in considering how citizens and officials in our own communities should behave. The opinion that our judges should sometimes ignore the law and try to replace it with better law is far from a stranger to law school classrooms and even political debates. It is not regarded as absurd in the special way it would be if people thought the connection between law and coercion so uncontroversial as to be conceptual in our present sense. This might seem to provide an overwhelming argument

---

23. G.W. Paton & D.P. Derham, A Textbook of Jurisprudence 316–17 (4th ed. 1972).

for positivist semantic theories of law in spite of the trouble I
have been trying to make for them.[24]

3. There are psychologists who delight in talking of an apperceptive
   mass. I am not quite sure what such an apperceptive mass may
   be, nor of whether it is at all. But I am very sure that these psychologists have a strong truth by the tail. The only question, as
   A.G. Keller used to put it, is whether, for all our firm grip to the
   tail, we shall have skill and patience to work up over the rump.
   The truth that we have seized upon is this: you see in your
   case almost exactly what you brought to it, and hardly more. If
   you bring much, you see much. If you bring nothing, that is
   what you see. A *little*, each case will add to what you knew. The
   measure of what it adds, again, is what you bring.[25]

In the first passage, we see a formal style, expressed partly by
technical terms (*juristic act* and *res mancipi*), partly by legalistic
phrasing (*the law cares not how the will be expressed, is strictly laid
down, the law may lay down that, signed writing attested by two witnesses*). Our being expected to know the meaning of the Latinism
res mancipi (= things transferable only by a formal ceremony of
conveyance) adds to the bookishness. The tone is staid, even dull,
an effect heightened by the absence of any human element until we
come to a direct mention of the *testator's wishes*.

The second passage contains none of the legal jargon that pervades
the first, though it expects us to be acquainted with *positivism*. The
use of the first person (*our, I*) relaxes the tone. The language here is
superficially simple, approximating the vocabulary of everyday English, though *wicked* is a little quaint. Despite its seeming simplicity,
the writing makes demands on us by requiring that we hold in mind
the prior discussion (*so uncontroversial as to be conceptual in our present sense, in the various ways we just noticed, in spite of the trouble I
have been trying to make for them* [i.e., semantic theories of law]).

---

24. RONALD DWORKIN, LAW'S EMPIRE 109 (1986).
25. KARL LLEWELLYN, THE BRAMBLE BUSH 56 (1930; repr. 1951).

The third passage is earthy. The writer not only uses the first person but also talks to us directly. The tone is unusually informal for legal writing. The writer's voice is everywhere apparent. He pokes fun at the vocabulary of psychologists and, one infers, disdains the jargon of lawyers. He uses the barnyard metaphor of having *truth by the tail* and trying to *work up over the rump*. The pace is leisurely, as the writer elaborates the ideas in the second paragraph one by one. The vocabulary is that of educated colloquial English.

Despite marked differences, the word choice in all three quotations is within acceptable limits for legal writing. The most formal passage is not impenetrably abstruse, nor is the least formal passage breezy or chummy. Most 20th-century legal writing lies somewhere between the first and the second examples; much of what will be written in the 21st century ought to approach the third. We might advantageously adopt a style more relaxed than the one that talks about "perceiving truths" and that wonders whether "we may ascertain with increasing certainty the extent and nature of those truths." For all that, we might better have truth by the tail and start working up over the rump.

GRAMMAR AND SYNTAX

2.21 Use the active voice.

Voice, in language, refers to the relationship between the subject and the verb in any sentence that has a direct object. If the subject performs the action of the verb, the sentence is active; if the subject is the recipient of the action, then it's passive. Here's the difference:

Active
The court reversed the judgment.

Passive
The judgment was reversed by the court.

The two sentences say essentially the same thing, but the focus differs, the emphasis has changed. The subject and the object swap places. Passively phrased sentences are often more abstract, since you need not mention the actor:

> The judgment was reversed.

Or, worse yet:

> Notice must be given.

Fine, but by whom? How much better to write:

> X must give notice.

The passive voice may lead merely to vagueness, but it also lends itself to obfuscation. For example, "A mistake was made" sounds like an attempt to conceal the blameworthy (the writer, no doubt?).

Even so, the passive results more often from lazy thinking than from deception. Whatever the cause, the passive can lead to problems, as when a federal judge observed: "The statute is not particularly helpful, since it speaks in the passive voice ('suits . . . may be brought'), and does not identify who can bring suit."[26]

The English-speaking reader expects a true sequence in actor, action, and recipient—as opposed to an inverted sequence—unless an inversion somehow improves the statement. Typically, changing a passive voice to active saves words and makes reading easier:

Not this:	But this:
The fee simple interest could have *been conveyed* by her to the defendant.	She could have conveyed the fee simple interest to the defendant.

---

26. Adkins v. General Motors Corp., 556 F. Supp. 452, 455 (S.D. Ohio 1983).

It *is not found* that defendant *was motivated* by an intent to destroy the value of plaintiff's interest in the promissory note, as *is alleged* in the complaint.	The court does not find that defendant intended to destroy the value of plaintiff's interest in the promissory note, as the complaint alleges.

In some contexts, of course, you may prefer the passive, as when the actor or agent is immaterial:

> The prisoner is to be executed at midnight. (No reason to mention the state employee who pulls the switch.)

> Several other books on the same subject were published that year. (No reason to name the publishers.)

Perhaps you want the sentence to focus on something other than the actor or agent:

> Appellant Gladys Lear was found guilty on two charges of "harboring a barking dog" ..., violation of which is a class "C" misdemeanor.[27]

To drag the jury in as the subject of that sentence would misplace the emphasis, now squarely on the wrongdoer.

Remember: by consistently using the active voice, you animate your style. But use the passive voice whenever you decide that the active would undesirably shift your emphasis or alter what you want to say.

2.22 Put pronouns in their proper case and number.

Personal pronouns take different forms as subject and object, and as singular and plural. The pronoun *he* becomes *him* as object, *who* becomes *whom*, and so on.

> Jerry had dinner *with Charles and me.*

---

27. Lear v. State, 753 S.W.2d 737, 738 (Tex. App.—Austin 1988).

There were differences *between him and me.*

The tortfeasor, the court found, *was he.*

We judges *are* to decide real cases, not hypothetical ones.

Assign this case to *whoever needs* more work.

We occasionally encounter gross errors:

Not this:	*But this:*
We need to confer with *whomever* worked on this project and then have *he* or *she* draft a motion for summary judgment.	We need to confer with *whoever* worked on this project and then have *him* or *her* draft a motion for summary judgment. [*Whoever* is the subject of *worked*; the phrase *him or her* is the compound object of *have.*]
Finally, the fault is said to lie in part with *we* "eccentric professors."	Finally, the fault is said to lie in part with *us* "eccentric professors." [*Us* because the pronoun acts as object of the preposition *with.*]

Reserve the reflexive pronoun *myself* exclusively for reflexive or intensive uses.

Not this:	*But this:*
All press inquiries should be directed to Diane or myself.	All press inquiries should be directed to Diane or me.
My wife and myself are delighted to be here.	My wife and I are delighted to be here.

Contexts properly requiring *myself* as a reflexive or intensive occur infrequently in legal writing:

I have decided that I must recuse myself. (reflexive)

I will limit myself to a few examples. (reflexive)

I myself have tried to respond to Justice Scalia's difficult questioning. (intensive)

Issues of gender have complicated the use of singular pronouns. Traditionally, words such as *either, everybody, anybody, neither, nobody,* and *someone* have acted as singular antecedents calling for *he* (or *she*).

Everybody here thinks *he* could give a rousing jury argument.

Neither a corporate lawyer nor a litigator should overlook the importance of properly maintaining *his* files.

Nobody would argue that *his* demeanor does not affect the judge's attitude toward *him.*

Some reformers have argued for considering these words plural— that is, replacing them to take *their* so as not to reinforce the masculine notions conjured up in our minds[28]—but formal English still treats the words as singular.[29] Masculine generic pronouns can often be avoided (see 7.15), and we should try to avoid them. But when you must use a pronoun to refer to a word such as *either* or *nobody* or *everyone*, make the pronoun singular—even if that means using an occasional *he or she.*

2.23 Make the verb agree in number with its subject.

A simple rule: plural subjects take plural verbs, and singular subjects take singular verbs. But many things in a sentence may divert the writer's eye. For example, "false attraction" occurs when a plural noun intervenes between a singular subject and the verb:

---

28. *See, e.g.,* Robert Eagleson, *A Singular Use of* They, 5 Scribes J. Legal Writing 87 (1994–1995).
29. *See* BRYAN A. GARNER, A DICTIONARY OF MODERN AMERICAN USAGE 240–41, 446–47, 528–29 (1998).

Not this:
This problem is also declining in importance as the *language* of statutes *are* modernized.

But this:
This problem is also declining in importance as the *language* of statutes *is* modernized. [The subject is the word *language*, not *statutes*.]

At first, the *difference* between McCormick and Wigmore—or between McCormick and any of the other writers mentioned here—*are* a bit startling.

At first, the *difference* between McCormick and Wigmore—or between McCormick and any of the other writers mentioned here—*is* a bit startling. [The subject is *difference*, not some compound of *McCormick, Wigmore,* and *other writers*.]

The appellate judge's immediate *audience are* his colleagues who sat with him when an appeal was argued.

The appellate judge's immediate *audience is* his colleagues who sat with him when an appeal was argued.

As in the final example just quoted, writers sometimes incorrectly look to the predicate rather than to the subject for the noun governing the verb. But the singular subject *audience* governs the verb, not the plural predicate (*his colleagues who sat with him . . .*).

These ills may be cured by adapting the most basic principle of golf: keep your eye on the subject.

2.24 Anchor modifiers to what they modify.

Misplaced modifiers come in various shapes and sizes. Among the most common is the participial phrase—that is, a phrase built on a participle (usually a verb form that ends in -*ing* or -*ed*). A participial phrase should be tied to the grammatical subject, which should appear unmistakably just before or after the phrase. A participle is misplaced when it appears to modify the wrong word. A participle "dangles" when the word it should modify does not appear in the sentence; in effect, the participle tries to sever its relationship with the noun and thus to become a preposition. "As enemies of the dangling participle well know, the English language does not always force a writer to specify which of two possible objects is the one to which a modifying phrase relates."[30]

Misplaced:

> *Gnawing* on the slipper, *the man* scolded the dog. (Grammatically, the sentence says that the man is doing the gnawing.)

Dangling:

> *Watching* the river, *the manikin* was spotted floating near the bank. (A neat trick for a manikin, to watch the river and float in it simultaneously. The participle "dangles" because the people watching the river do not appear in the sentence.)

Of course, the writer of those sentences meant to say:

> The man scolded the *dog, gnawing* on the slipper.

> While *watching* the river, *someone* spotted the manikin floating near the bank.

Mispositioned words cause grammatical blunders and ambiguity. Perhaps the most common grammatical error in judicial opinions is this one, born of a desire to avoid the first person:

Not this:	*But this:*
Finding no error, *the judgment* of the trial court is affirmed. (Dangling participle)	*Finding* no error, *we affirm* the judgment of the trial court.
Applying those principles to the facts of this case, it is clear that the plaintiffs cannot recover. (Dangling participle)	*If we apply those principles to the facts of this case, it* is clear that the plaintiffs cannot recover.

---

30. Young v. Community Nutrition Inst., 476 U.S. 974, 980–81 (1986) (per O'Connor, J.).

The dangler in that first example results from the passive voice (*the judgment . . . is affirmed*) in place of the active (*we affirm the judgment*). In the second example, the dangler results from the lack of a person in the sentence to do the *applying*; the sentence contains merely the expletive (or "dummy word") *it* after the initial phrase.

A few words that are technically danglers are now accepted as prepositions by virtue of long-standing usage:

Barring any unforeseen change in the evidence, the defendant ought to prevail in her claim of adverse possession.

Considering the sentiments expressed by several powerful legislators, the legislation will probably pass.

Judging from the public outcry, the legislators must feel a great deal of pressure to take a stand on the issue.

Regarding the issue of criminal intent, there is insufficient evidence for the court to find that it existed here.

Other acceptable danglers are *according, concerning, owing* (*to*), *respecting, speaking,* and *taking* (usually *account of, into account*).

Participles are not the only troublesome modifiers. Words such as *only* (see pp. 130–31) require careful placement. And "squinting modifiers" appear ambiguously between two sentence elements, either of which might be modified.

That the court neglected this issue *completely* undermines the authority of its ruling.

Because *completely* might refer either to *neglected* or to *undermines,* the sentence needs revision:

That the court *completely neglected* this issue undermines the authority of its ruling.

Or:

That the court neglected this issue *undermines completely* the authority of its ruling.

Or yet again:

> It *completely undermines* the authority of the ruling that the court neglected this issue.

Think carefully about what words are affected by a modifier.

2.25 Split infinitives warily, if at all.

H.W. Fowler, the greatest 20th-century authority on English usage, divided the English-speaking world into five classes: (1) those who neither know nor care what a split infinitive is; (2) those who do not know, but care very much; (3) those who know and condemn; (4) those who know and approve; and (5) those who know and distinguish. It is to this last class that we should aspire. The aspiration requires a good ear, without which the best course is to avoid all splits.

An infinitive is the tenseless form of a verb preceded by *to*, as in *to reverse* or *to modify*. You split the infinitive when you place one or more words between *to* and the verb, as in *to summarily reverse* or *to unwisely modify*.

Most split infinitives should be avoided. Here is an example of the capricious split, which serves no purpose (apart from jarring the reader):

> It is not necessary *to here enlarge* upon this point.

As with so many other examples, we can easily correct the split:

> It is not necessary here *to enlarge* upon this point.

Or:

> It is not necessary *to enlarge* upon this point here.

The difficult questions arise when you come upon a sentence like this one:

> He hopes *to more than double* his profits in the next three quarters.

The only way around splitting the infinitive is to reword the sentence entirely, as by writing:

> He hopes that his profits will more than double in the next three quarters.

The revision ever so slightly changes the emphasis, however, because *he* no longer seems to be the agent directly responsible for the increase.

Justified splits aren't uncommon. They merely require the ability that Fowler wrote of: the ability to distinguish. *To flatly state* suggests something different from *to state flatly*. That's a question of nuance. But sometimes nuance doesn't matter, and the only natural phrasing requires a split infinitive:

> The majority improperly places on the appellees the burden *to affirmatively establish* the existence of a statutory exception.

> The statute prohibits supplying others with the necessary information and documents *to falsely claim* their income as tax-exempt.

Avoiding either split while retaining the infinitive would ruin the sentence. Usually the worst fix is to put the adverb before the infinitive (*affirmatively to establish, falsely to claim*, etc.).

If you can't avoid awkwardness, and don't have a good ear, then avoid having adverbs modify infinitives altogether. For example, in place of the examples just quoted, you might write:

> The majority improperly places on the appellees the burden of affirmatively establishing the existence of a statutory exemption.

> The statute prohibits supplying others with the necessary information and documents for falsely claiming their income as tax-exempt.

2.26 Don't be afraid to begin a sentence with *And* or *But.*

Even in the most formal prose, you may use *And* or *But* to begin a sentence. It has always been so. Follow the lead of Justice Holmes:

Courts proceed step by step. And we now have to consider whether the cautious statement in the former case marked the limit of the law . . . .[31]

But to many people the superfluous is the necessary, and it seems to me that Government does not go beyond its sphere in attempting to make life livable for them.[32]

You needn't worry that you're bending a rule: look up the point in any grammar book. More to the point, look at first-rate prose: you'll find that professional writers typically use *And* and *But* as sentence-starters with great frequency. But avoid a great many consecutive sentences beginning with one of these conjunctions.

2.27 End sentences with prepositions when you need to.

Winston Churchill gave what we should all regard as the final word on this subject. When scolded for ending a sentence with a preposition, Churchill rejoined, "That is the type of arrant pedantry up with which I shall not put." H.W. Fowler himself called the schoolmarm's rule against prepositions at the end a "cherished superstition."[33]

Blasting the "rule" does not mean that you want to make a sentence end with four prepositions:

That is a good book to be read to out of from.

But don't go to great lengths to avoid the preposition at the end, as by always writing:

The peculiarities of legal English are often used as a stick with which to beat the official.

instead of:

---

31. Johnson v. United States, 228 U.S. 457, 458 (1913) (per Holmes, J.).
32. Tyson & Brother v. Banton, 273 U.S. 418, 447 (1927) (Holmes, J., dissenting).
33. H.W. FOWLER, A DICTIONARY OF MODERN ENGLISH USAGE 457 (1926).

The peculiarities of legal English are often used as a stick to beat the official with.[34]

The spurious rule is a remnant of Latin grammar, which does not control English grammar. If it may be called a rule, it is a rule of rhetoric and not of syntax, the idea being to end sentences with strong words, not weak ones. That principle is sound (see 3.5), but not to the extent of disallowing every exception. Remember: prepositions are not necessarily bad words to end sentences with.

2.28 Use conditional sentences instead of provisos.

Readers should never discover that they have been misreading because the author has held back important facts. When you habitually say, "Such and such is true, *provided that* it is not true in these instances," you spring an unpleasant surprise on your readers. You have ended by contradicting the blanket statement you made in your opening thrust. And you've probably allowed your sentence to sprawl. You're asking your readers to study your sentence, not just to read it:

> No person who has not attained the age of 16 years may apply for a driver's license, *provided that*, if any such person who has attained the age of 14 years demonstrates to the Highway Department that not having a license will create a genuine hardship, such person shall be eligible to apply.

It's usually much better to lead in by stating under what conditions the statement holds true, by using the conditional *if.* In ridding the sentence of the proviso, we make the two negatives in the opening clause unnecessary:

> A person 16 years of age or older may apply for a driver's license. If a person 14 or 15 years old wishes to apply, he or she must demon-

---

34. ERNEST GOWERS, PLAIN WORDS: THEIR ABC 13 (1954).

strate to the Highway Department that not having a driver's license will create a genuine hardship.

It's also possible to write the sentence without the conditional *if:*

A person 16 years of age or older may apply for a driver's license. A person 14 or 15 years old is also eligible to apply, but only upon demonstrating to the Highway Department that not having a driver's license will create a genuine hardship.

The phrase *provided that* has no real place in good legal drafting.[35] Banning the phrase from legal writing would benefit us all.

---

35. *See* BRYAN A. GARNER, LEGAL WRITING IN PLAIN ENGLISH § 36, at 107–12 (2001).

THREE

Fundamental Principles of Legal Writing

3.1 Brevity and Clarity

Ideally, legal writing is taut. To tighten your style, try to cut one-fourth of every sentence in your first draft. Strike out every slack syllable. In his brilliant statement of facts in *Palsgraf*, Cardozo referred to *a package of small size;*[1] he might better have written *a small package.*

Make every word tell. Rooting out verbiage isn't easy; verbosity often results from quick, facile writing. Watch out for recurrent phrases that are the verbal equivalent of throat-clearing; for example:

In my considered opinion, ...

May I respectfully suggest that . . . .

I should note here that it would be helpful to remember the fact that . . . .

It should not be forgotten that . . . .

It is also of importance to bear in mind the following considerations . . . .

---

1. Palsgraf v. Long Island R.R., 162 N.E. 99, 99 (N.Y. 1928).

Consideration should be given to the possibility of carrying into effect . . . .

These needless buildups wrap the reader's mind in wool before the point can be made. Forget the opening flourish and say what you mean. Take some typical examples of pompous indirection:

Not this:

In large part, it was our anticipation of this type of claim which cautioned us for so long against abrogation of the immunity rule.

But this:

Our anticipation of such claims long cautioned us against abrogating the immunity rule.

Not this:

It is to be noted that in this case the amended petition upon which the judgment was rendered for Smith was to recover a debt owing by the defendant arising from the purchase of the same oil and for the same prices as alleged in the original petition, and judgment was rendered for exactly the same sum as was sought to be recovered in both petitions.

But this:

Notably, the debt that Smith recovered under the amended petition was the same debt as she sought in the original petition.

Occasionally, cutting your sentence down will produce brevity but not clarity. For example, you might begin with this:

A will is ambulatory in character and subject to change or revocation at any time.

You realize that *ambulatory* means "subject to change or revocation," so you pare down the sentence:

A will is ambulatory.

The problem is that many readers won't understand *ambulatory*, which is legal jargon. So you might write instead:

> A will may be changed or revoked at any time before the testator dies.

This revision uses more words but is more immediately comprehensible to many more readers.

In law, wordy sentences like those just quoted are hardly more common than those that rip their seams:

> This, we may add, limited to restrictions imposed by terms of the ordinance relating to the use of land or the location and character of buildings that may be located thereon, even in the absence of provisions in the contract excepting them, must necessarily be his position, for we are convinced, although it must be conceded there are some decisions to the contrary, the rule supported by the better reasoned decisions, indeed if not by the great weight of authority, is that municipal restrictions of such character, existing at the time of the execution of a contract for the sale of real estate, are not such encumbrances or burdens on title as may be availed of by a vendee to avoid his agreement to purchase on the ground they render his title unmerchantable.[2]

The important information in that 133-word sentence boils down to 19 or 20 words, as in these two versions:

> A purchaser cannot use municipal restrictions such as these to void the contract on grounds of an unmerchantable title.

> A purchaser cannot void the contract by saying that the title is unmerchantable because of municipal restrictions such as these.

Most of the original sentence is dross, to be tossed on the second-draft slag heap.

Beware also of the standard flotsam phrases, which float idly in a

---

2. Lohmeyer v. Bower, 227 P.2d 102, 108 (Kan. 1951).

sentence without carrying any of the meaning. There is usually no reason to write *it seems to me that, in terms of, on a* _____ *basis, my sense is that, in the first instance,* or *the fact that.* Think thrice about whether your readers need these space-fillers.

State your thoughts positively, not negatively. Rather than:

The decision was not wrong.

write:

The decision was correct.

Instead of *increasing deemphasis,* say *decreasing emphasis.* Likewise, when the context allows:

Not this:	*But this:*
did not have support	lacked support
did not recall	forgot
not apposite	inapposite
not current	outdated
not important	unimportant; trivial
not on purpose	accidental
of no use	useless

Don't indulge in the detestable habit of shoving several negatives together. Even lawyers have a hard time decoding a sentence like this one:

The order vacated had required the oil companies to abstain from refusing to deliver interstate shipments of oil.

The sentence really says something simple:

Until vacated, the order had required the oil companies to deliver interstate shipments of oil.

Be specific and concrete. Instead of:

Ms. Jones returned to her apartment and discovered indications that it had been burglarized. She contacted the authorities.

Write:

> When Ms. Jones returned to her apartment, she found her front
> door ajar, the lock broken. Inside, she saw that her stereo, television,
> and jewelry box had been taken. Within two minutes, she called the
> police.

Even in abstract arguments, concrete illustrations hammer down
the point, as when Holmes explained the nub of legal intention:
"even a dog distinguishes between being stumbled over and being
kicked."[3]

Give enough supporting detail, but avoid excessive detail. You
must not, in the misconceived pursuit of completeness, bury your
readers under facts. Legal writers often slavishly recite one date
after another in a chronological narrative. When the dates are incidental, instead of saying, "On June 24, 2001," say, "Early last summer." You ought to "suppress much and omit more . . . . [O]mit
what is tedious or irrelevant, and suppress what is tedious and necessary."[4] Still, good writers eagerly retain facts that serve a variety
of purposes. Keep whatever expedites the argument, builds up the
reasoning, or strikes home the legal and moral principles involved.

3.2 Simplicity of Structure

Structure your thoughts simply and directly. If you don't, readers
will respond much as Justice William Maule once did in listening
to an advocate:

> Mr. Smith, do you not think by introducing a little order into your
> narrative you might possibly render yourself a trifle more intelligi-
> ble? It may be my fault that I cannot follow you—I know that my
> brain is getting dilapidated; but I should like to stipulate for some
> sort of order. There are plenty of them. There is the chronological,

---

3. OLIVER WENDELL HOLMES, THE COMMON LAW 7 (1881; repr. 1963).
4. ROBERT LOUIS STEVENSON, LEARNING TO WRITE 27 (1888; repr. 1920).

the botanical, the metaphysical, the geographical, even the alphabet-
ical order would be better than no order at all.[5]

To order your ideas sensibly, you'll need to begin your journey
with an itinerary, however sketchy. True, not everyone has a knack
for outlining. But just as you wouldn't go on a cross-continental
trip without a road map, you shouldn't start writing sentences and
paragraphs before you have a plan for the entire piece. If you begin
with a fairly detailed outline, you're better able to know the relevance of what you write in any given section. And you help ensure
that you reach your conclusion only after working through all the
necessary steps.

Structurally, the most prominent positions in a unit of writing—whether a sentence, a paragraph, or an entire book—are the
beginning and the end. Irving Younger used to lecture about the
principles of primacy and recency in closing argument: juries remember what comes first in the argument and what comes last.
With one significant exception that we'll come to shortly, these
principles apply to units of legal writing. Concentrate on how you
begin and end each sentence, each paragraph, each letter, each
multivolume treatise.

3.3   Organizing Arguments

Brief-writers usually follow an issue-by-issue arrangement, though
a looser structure may be appropriate for an essay or journal article. Issue-by-issue arrangement orders thought logically, so that
structure reveals the sequence of thinking or the merit of the
points under discussion. Critical argument usually progresses in
this way:

1. Stating the issues
2. Stating the facts

---

5. Maule, J. (as quoted in NORMAN BIRKETT, SIX GREAT ADVOCATES 106–07 (1961)).

3. Explaining the legal premises involved in the first (most important) issue
4. Marshaling the critical evidence on the first issue
5. Weighing the conflicting evidence on the first issue
6. Resolving the conflicts on the first issue in the advocate's favor
7. Explaining the legal premises involved in the second issue
8. Marshaling the critical evidence on the second issue
9. Weighing the conflicting evidence on the second issue
10. Resolving the conflicts on the second issue in the advocate's favor
11. Urging a particular conclusion

The order might vary to suit your immediate purpose. What you want to avoid is the type of argument that, say, jumps straight into the evidence—while the reader doesn't yet know what to focus on—then points out discrepancies in the evidence, then raises an issue and posits a verdict, then rejects unfavorable evidence, and finally restates the verdict.

In what order should you take up issues? That is a question *you* must decide. Don't let others do it for you. Lawyers too often allow their opponents to dictate the order of arguments; naturally, an opponent's order usually favors the opponent. You should order your own arguments according to how you have framed the issues. Likewise, judges need not follow the argumentative pattern of advocates; judges ought to adjudicate the issues in what strikes them as the best, most logical order.

Books on rhetoric commonly touch on this issue as it relates to advocacy, the traditional advice being: "As a general rule, in presenting our own arguments we should not descend from our strongest arguments to our weakest . . . ."[6] We don't want to leave the audience, it is said, with a bad impression. Instead, "if we have

---

6. EDWARD P.J. CORBETT, CLASSICAL RHETORIC FOR THE MODERN STUDENT 322 (2d ed. 1971).

available to us a number of relatively strong and weak arguments, we might find it best to start out with a strong argument, then slip in some of the weaker arguments, and then end up with the strongest argument."[7]

This advice may be useful to the oral advocate, but not to the brief-writer. For one thing, this reasoning applies to speech more than to writing, "since the listener, unlike the reader, cannot skip ahead or go back."[8] But most important, to end with the strongest point would flout the conventions of brief-writing. Judges expect to see your best arguments first. And they are used to seeing two-page "throwaway" sections at the end of a brief. (If the arguments are truly throwaway, then throw them away.) When judges come to the weak points in a brief, they may assume that you won't raise anything else of importance.

In argumentative writing, then, beware the rhetorician's advice. True, the conclusion is an emphatic point, but less so in legal advocacy than in other types of writing.

Commonsense ordering of arguments requires that related issues be kept together. If two sections of a brief deal with whether the judgment below is appealable, two with comity, and two with attorneys' fees, keep the related sections together. If you represent the appellee and you want to defeat appealability, you might choose to place the arguments on that issue first—as if the court need not reach the other issues because the case isn't properly on appeal. If you represent the appellant and you feel confident that the appeal is proper, you might put the appealability arguments last: not as throwaway arguments, of course, but as strong punches that keep you in court for the arguments on the merits.

One rule of structure is ironclad: the capital importance of the openers. The opening paragraph gets the subject underway; it

---

7. *Id.*
8. RICHARD A. POSNER, LAW AND LITERATURE: A MISUNDERSTOOD RELATION 297 (1988).

must engage readers, make them want to stay the course. A weak opener weakens all that follows. Here, for example, is an apologetic opener from an article that begs to go unread:

> This article examines some of the literature on the interpretation of constitutionally guaranteed rights. The conclusions are enumerated at the end of the article. They may appear rather banal to those who have been following the literature on rights. The reader may wish to consult the conclusions before deciding finally to embark on the journey through the intervening text.

Given the writer's invitation to scant the text, who would venture to slog through it?

Granted, some subjects have a more immediate appeal than others. Even so, the stylist searches for an approach—often rejecting several approaches before finally settling on one—that will draw the reader into the text. For example, judicial opinions involving domicile and probate often blunt the reader's attention. They need not. See how effectively this opening paragraph stimulates your curiosity to read further:

> Errol Flynn was a film actor whose performance gave pleasure to many millions. On June 10, 1909, he was born in Hobart, Tasmania; and on Oct. 14, 1959, he died in Vancouver, British Columbia. When he was seventeen he was expelled from school in Sydney; and in the next thirty-three years he lived a life [that] was full, lusty, restless and colourful. In his career, in his three marriages, in his friendships, in his quarrels, and in bed with the many women he took there, he lived with zest and irregularity. The lives of film stars are not cast in the ordinary mould; and in some respects Errol Flynn's was more stellar than most. When he died, he posed the only question that I have to decide: Where was he domiciled at the date of his death?[9]

That the subject is Errol Flynn's estate adds intrinsic interest; but the opinion might just as easily have begun in the tedious, worka-

---

9. Re Flynn, [1968] 1 All Eng. Rev. 49, 50 (Ch.D.) (per Megarry, J.).

day manner to which legal readers have become inured. Note how the paragraph roughly follows the age-old paradigm for the opening paragraph of a theme: an inverted pyramid that begins with a general statement, progresses through sentences of greater particularity, and culminates in a focused statement of the thesis or question presented. That paradigm is not always the most appropriate model; here, however, it would be hard to improve on.

3.4   Constructing Paragraphs

A paragraph marks the full development of a single idea; it develops a unit of thought that moves the reader toward a conclusion. Especially when revising your prose, pay close attention to the movement within individual paragraphs. If you've made two major points in a single paragraph or have included something extraneous to the idea you're developing, divide or cut.

Paragraphs may be short or long. As a rule, make your paragraphs more than one sentence but less than a full page. Still, one-sentence paragraphs aren't forbidden. Occasionally they serve as good transitional devices, as with the middle paragraph here:

> We are able thus to delude ourselves by giving "reasons" for our attitudes. When challenged by ourselves or others to justify our positions or our conduct, we manufacture *ex post facto* a host of "principles" which we induce ourselves to believe are conclusions reasoned out by logical processes from actual facts in the actual world. So we persuade ourselves that our lives are governed by Reason.
>
> This practice of making ourselves appear, to ourselves and others, more rational than we are, has been termed "rationalization."
>
> Rationalization not only conceals the real foundations of our biased beliefs but also enables us to maintain, side by side as it were, beliefs which are inherently incompatible. For many of our biased beliefs are contradicted by other beliefs . . . . [10]

---

10. JEROME FRANK, LAW AND THE MODERN MIND 32 (1930; repr. 1963).

As for conventional longer paragraphs, build each one around a topic sentence. R.J. Tresolini provides a model in the following paragraph from *Justice and the Supreme Court.* The first sentence, a generalization, finds specific support in each sentence that follows it. Tresolini includes nothing extraneous to the idea he develops:

> No justice of the Supreme Court has been more roundly denounced and so grossly misrepresented as was Roger Brooke Taney. He was bitterly condemned on various occasions during his many years in public life. Even his death failed to halt the torrent of unbridled criticism. Upon hearing of Taney's death in 1864, Charles Francis Adams wrote jubilantly to Henry Adams: "So old Taney is at last dead . . . the darling wish of Taney's last day is doomed not to be realized. It was not reserved for him to put the veto of law on the Proclamation of Emancipation." Congress refused to pass a bill providing funds for a Taney bust in the courtroom. In opposing the bill, Charles Sumner rose on the Senate floor to proclaim, "The name of Taney is to be hooted down the page of history. Judgment is beginning now; and an emancipated country will fasten upon him the stigma which he deserves . . . . He administered justice at least wickedly, and degraded the judiciary of the country, and degraded the age."[11]

Every paragraph ought to work this way. Of course, you won't always want an assertion followed by supporting details—you might instead draw the conclusion at the end, after the particulars that lead up to it. Your approach depends on the relationship of the ideas contained in the paragraph. But the possibilities here are finite.

In fact, there are nine common ways to develop paragraphs.

Pattern	*Method*
1. assertion, then details	argument, exposition
2. cause and effect	argument, narration, exposition
3. likeness, analogy	argument, exposition

---

11. R.J. TRESOLINI, JUSTICE AND THE SUPREME COURT 7–8 (1963).

Pattern	Method
4. contrast	argument, exposition
5. data, then conclusion	exposition, narration
6. chronology	narration
7. definition	exposition
8. classification	exposition
9. particulars in spatial order	description

Whatever the approach, the ideas should unfold sensibly, with unity and coherence. Readers should not have to reorder sentences in their minds to follow your reasoning.

In a factual narrative, the paragraphing often follows a temporal sequence, as in the first of the following quoted paragraphs. In the second paragraph, a temporal transition leads to the topic sentence, as assertion, followed by details; in the third, the topic sentence, another assertion, is followed by evidence supporting it. The writer progresses from narration to exposition.

> One summer evening in 1977, a suburban Chicago police officer spotted Cathleen Crowell, a young employee of a local fast food restaurant, wandering down a deserted street. Even from his patrol car, the officer could see something was wrong. Crowell was shaking; her gait was aimless and stumbling. Her clothing was ripped and soiled, and she seemed to be bruised. When the officer asked whether she needed help, Crowell said she had been raped.
>
> Crowell was taken to the hospital for examination and treatment, and later she was questioned. Everything seemed to point to rape. Her body was scraped and bruised, and she had a large bump on the back of her head. She had external and internal genital injuries. There was a large stain on her underwear that later proved to be seminal fluid.
>
> Crowell's conduct also was consistent with her rape story. She seemed traumatized. She huddled in a corner, crying and shivering. She was terrified by men and refused to be questioned by them. She clung to a policewoman, digging her nails into the officer's arm.[12]

---

12. Margaret Frossard, *When the Accuser Recants: People v. Dotson,* 14 LITIGATION 11, 11 (Summer 1988).

Paragraphing should also show the progression from one idea to the next. At the outset of each paragraph, orient the reader with a transitional connective or signpost. We have three means of providing such a transition: (1) the transitional words and phrases commonly used for this purpose, (2) pointing words (such as *this* or *that*), and (3) echo links (words and phrases that refer notionally to what has preceded). Often these techniques work in combination.

Among the standard words used for transitional purposes are *but, and, besides, even so, further, moreover, nevertheless, still, therefore, thus, yet.* For example, Tresolini might have followed the paragraph quoted on p. 63 with these two paragraphs:

> Shortly after his death, an article in the *Atlantic Monthly* said that Taney was disposed "to serve the cause of evil." [Examples of Taney's infamy complete the paragraph.]
>
> But it is now clear that the judgment of his detractors will not prevail. [Discussion of recent scholarship completes the paragraph.]

If we were to make the transition by means of a pointing word and an echo link, we might say:

> Shortly after his death, an article in the *Atlantic Monthly* said that Taney was disposed "to serve the cause of evil." [Additional contemporary judgments complete the paragraph.]
>
> Though this unflattering picture of Taney persisted for many years, it is now clear that the judgment of his detractors will not prevail. . . . [Discussion of recent scholarship completes the paragraph.]

Yet Tresolini used neither of these versions. Instead, he combined all three methods to make a strong transition.

> Shortly after his death, an article in the *Atlantic Monthly* said that Taney was disposed "to serve the cause of evil." . . .
>
> But though this unflattering picture of Taney persisted for many years, it is now clear that the judgment of his detractors will not prevail. . . .

Linking your paragraphs keeps the reader with you. While writing, experiment with pointing words, echo links, and transitional words to develop greater versatility in moving from one idea to another. Then, while revising, check to see that the transitions are on the page and not just in your own mind.

3.5 Constructing Sentences

It is only a slight exaggeration to say that a "sentence must be so written that the punch word comes at the end."[13] That the end is emphatic explains why periodic sentences (see 6.13) work. For example:

> But when for the first time I was called to speak on such an occasion as this, the only thought that could come into my mind, the only feeling that could fill my heart, the only words that could spring to my lips, were a hymn to her in whose name we are met here tonight—to our mistress, the Law.[14]

An unimportant phrase at the end makes a sentence fizzle:

Not this:
The plaintiffs caused the losses with but a few exceptions.

But this:
With but a few exceptions, the plaintiffs caused the losses.

The witness first testified graphically about the crime scene, even opining that the two victims had been dueling each other in the expansive back yard, the implication being that only the two decedents were involved, but right before the climactic part of the description the testimony ended in a flurry of motions to strike and various collateral matters that the judge took duly under advisement, including lead counsel's long-standing plans for a vacation at a golf resort.

Though the day was plagued with procedural motions, some important testimony did emerge: the witness testified graphically about the crime scene, even opining that the two victims had been dueling each other in the expansive back yard. The implication was that no one else was involved.

The beginning of the sentence is likewise emphatic. In the sequence just quoted from Holmes, the phrase *first time* lingers as we continue through the sentence to the emphatic end. Look how *those who believe* remain present throughout this sentence by Justice Holmes:

> But to those who believe with me that not the least godlike of man's activities is the large survey of causes, that to know is not less than to feel, I say—and I say no longer with any doubt—that a man may live greatly in the law as well as elsewhere; that there as well as elsewhere his thought may find its unity in an infinite perspective; that there as well as elsewhere he may wreak himself upon life, may drink the bitter cup of heroism, may wear his heart out after the unattainable.[15]

The principles of emphasis are easily visible in these longish sentences, but they apply to sentences of any length. Watch the words at the ends and the beginnings of even your shortest sentences.

> Law is the cement of society and also an essential medium of change.[16]

> No answer is what the wrong question begets.[17]

Speaking of short sentences, lawyers frequently overlook that paragon of directness, the simple declarative sentence. Observe how Ronald Dworkin, a lucid and graceful theorist, opens *Law's Empire*:

> It matters how judges decide cases. It matters most to people unlucky or litigious or wicked or saintly enough to find themselves in court.[18]

13. Karl Llewellyn, *A Lecture on Appellate Advocacy*, 29 U. Chi. L. Rev. 627, 628 (1962).
14. Oliver Wendell Holmes, *The Law*, *in* COLLECTED LEGAL PAPERS 25, 28 (1920; repr. 1952).
15. Oliver Wendell Holmes, *The Profession of the Law*, *in* COLLECTED LEGAL PAPERS 29, 30 (1920; repr. 1952).
16. GLANVILLE WILLIAMS, LEARNING THE LAW 1 (11th ed. 1982).
17. JOHN HART ELY, DEMOCRACY AND DISTRUST 72 (1980).
18. RONALD DWORKIN, LAW'S EMPIRE 1 (1986).

From that beginning, we are drawn through development of the argument in all its rich variety for another 413 pages. Throughout, Dworkin treats his readers to declarative sentences that say precisely what he means. He needs no cumbersome qualifications; he has no ill-fitting afterthoughts; he uses no obscure syntax to discuss jurisprudence. The same was true of William Prosser, who sometimes wrote startlingly simple sentences: "Causation is a fact. It is a matter of what has in fact occurred."[19]

Good sentences lack the excess bulk that most writers feel tempted to throw in. Those who succumb often suffer from the "*of*-and-*which* disease," a common sign of excessive formality and too much passive voice. The prepositions and relative pronouns and articles—the mortar holding our sentences together—engulf the few bricks they are supposed to cement together, as here:

> The gist of the opinion of the court of appeals, which was sitting en banc, was expressed in terms of the effect of the statutory immunity from suit, which had not been amended since the passage of the act by Congress in 1928.

We simplify the sentence by eliminating the excess mortar—one relative clause, several prepositions, and three passives:

> In its opinion, the en banc court of appeals relied on the statutory immunity, which Congress had not amended since passing the act in 1928.

Sentences larded with prepositions signal that you're trying to pack in too much information. Readers of legal prose often find themselves unable to get any air as they're sucked into verbal quicksand:

> Also of importance, without Ms. Stanlin's testimony that lawn mowers were actually missing from the Four Seasons store, it is doubtful that the delivery by the driver (even if he was Marshall) of two boxes,

---

19. WILLIAM L. PROSSER, THE LAW OF TORTS § 41, at 237 (4th ed. 1971).

of unknown content, showed that two lawn mowers, or any, were dropped off at Frederick Street, even though one of the (perhaps previously discarded) boxes indicated that, at least at one time, a lawn mower had been contained within it.

We can recast the sentence by breaking it up into three and cutting the inessential parts. We still don't have a work of art, but we certainly have an improvement:

> Ms. Stanlin testified that the lawn mowers were missing from the store. Apart from her testimony, the [plaintiff] had no proof that the mowers had been there. The driver's testimony that he delivered two boxes, not knowing their contents, does not alone prove their presence.

Problems crop up also at the other extreme—where prepositions are rarities—in what is called noun plague, or noun-banging. When more than two nouns follow in succession, the sentence becomes less readable.

Not this:	*But this:*
Consumers complained to their representatives about the National Highway Traffic Safety Administration automobile seatbelt interlock rule.	Consumers complained to their representatives about the "interlock" rule for automobile seatbelts, a rule applied by the National Highway Traffic Safety Administration.

Who knows what the following sentence is trying to say?

> The direct participation programs principal category of registration is the minimum qualification requirement for persons whose supervisory functions are limited to direct participation programs.

Here's a stab at revision:

> Those whose supervisory functions are limited to programs involving direct participation must first register for the programs.

Legal writers often land themselves in a mire of syntactic repetition. They typically start every sentence with the subject, as by writing:

> The Court, in the course of the hearing, noted that the accident had occurred in Randall County. The Court found that it was a proper forum in which to try the issues. The Court therefore denied the motion to transfer venue.

Instead of always beginning with the subject (*The Court*), try beginning with the subordinate clause (*in the course of the hearing*), so as to keep related words together:

> In the course of the hearing, the Court noted that the accident had occurred in Randall County. The Court therefore ruled that it could properly try the issues and denied the motion to transfer venue.

I have casually used the phrase *subordinate clause*. The art of subordination—of knowing what to make less important and what more important—requires a constant attention to the ranking of ideas. If we simply set forth with equal emphasis all the ideas that come up, our writing becomes murky. But if we grammatically subordinate the lesser ideas to the greater—by putting the lesser ideas in dependent clauses and the greater in main clauses—readers follow our lead with greater ease and understanding. The writing gains clarity, economy, and emphasis.

We subordinate ideas by placing them in subordinate clauses, which begin with conjunctions such as *after, although, as, because, before, if, so that, until, when, while*. For example:

> When the judge entered the courtroom, everybody rose.

The result is termed a "complex sentence"—that is, one containing both a principal clause (*everybody rose*) and a subordinate clause (*When the judge entered the courtroom*).

A "compound sentence," by contrast, contains two or more principal clauses. It expresses ideas coordinately, without subordinating one idea to another:

> The judge entered the courtroom, and everybody rose.

Depending on the context, either version might be appropriate. But the complex sentence more clearly expresses the relationship between the judge's entering the room and everybody's rising.

More often than not, thoughts are complex rather than compound. Stating ideas as if they were all on the same level fails to account for the connections between them. Graceless writers often string together ideas with *and*, not fully employing the syntactic variety of our language.

If you use a complex sentence, put the principal idea in the main clause, not in the subordinate clause. The word *when* often introduces clauses that are wrongly subordinated:

Not this:	*But this:*
They were driving north when suddenly from around a curve a car crashed into them.	As they were driving north, suddenly from around a curve a car crashed into them.
The terrorist fell asleep after several hours, when the hostage crept away to safety.	When the terrorist fell asleep after several hours, the hostage crept away to safety.

Whether ideas are of equal or unequal importance, you can clarify their relationship through parallel phrasing. Our many parallel coordinators work to best advantage in longer sentences:

although/yet

both/and

either/or

first/second/third[20]

if/then[21]

just as/so

---

20. *See* 4.8.
21. *See* 2.28.

neither/nor[22]

not/but

not only/but also

not only/but . . . as well

when/then

where/there[23]

Watch the grammatical units framed by these connectives. If the sentence parts don't match, the result is a nonparallel construction (always to be avoided). Write *He did neither X nor Y*, not *He neither did X nor Y*, because, in the latter example, the phrases joined by *neither* and *nor* don't match.

Not this:
Easements can either be affirmative or negative.

The jury may have concluded that the entranceway was neither negligently constructed nor maintained by the Investment Company.

Judicial impartiality is not only a matter of constitutional law, but also public policy.

But this:
Easements can be either affirmative or negative.

The jury may have concluded that the entranceway was neither negligently constructed nor negligently maintained by the Investment Company. [Note that in the original sentence, omission of the word *negligently* in the second phrase exactly reverses the intended sense.]

Judicial impartiality is a matter not only of constitutional law, but also of public policy.

---

22. *See* Chapter 5, *nor*, pp. 128–29.
23. *See* 6.19 for an example from Karl Llewellyn's *The Bramble Bush.*

The attorney argued that there were mitigating circumstances, including the fact that the drug had been prescribed for Jones, who had completed a drug rehabilitation program, and Jones was no longer addicted.

The attorney argued three mitigating circumstances. First, Jones's doctor had prescribed the drug. Second, Jones had completed a drug-rehabilitation program. And third, he was no longer addicted.

FOUR

Some Matters of Form

4.1 Titles

> One begins by choosing a title, in order to assure oneself that one has
> a subject: for a title is a kind of substitute or shadow of a subject.
>
> *T.S. Eliot*[1]

Good legal writers try to make their titles short, straightforward, and punchy. Practicing lawyers, it is true, seldom need bother much about titling their work, although they may justifiably pause to consider whether to use *Motion to Vacate* instead of *Motion for Vacatur*. (To be plain, use the former.) Those who publish, however, must pay close attention to titles, since in titles the afflictions of legal writing can become virulently concentrated. Thus:

> *The Effects of Procedural Aspects and Outcome Salience on Procedural Fairness Judgments,* 2 Soc. Just. Res. 289 (1988).

> *Artistotle and Lyndon Baines Johnson: Thirteen Ways of Looking at Blackbirds and Nonprofit Corporations—The American Bar Association's Revised Model Nonprofit Corporation Act,* 39 Case W. Res. L. Rev. 751 (1988–1989).

---

1. "Scylla and Charybdis" (1952), *in* 23 Agenda 5 (1985).

It Happened to the Soviets and It Can Happen to You, Too: Compliance Considerations in the Context of an Emerging Bureaucratic Paradigm Shift, 1057 PLI/Corp. 1007 (June–July 1998).

The first of these is so abstractly phrased that you can barely glimpse even the broad subject area. You have to wonder whether reading the article really will increase your knowledge about the effects of procedural aspects of whatever. As to the second, with every word in that title, the article grows less inviting. Does the writer have a subject? The third title is weighed down with hyperbole, vague words, and vogue words; the topic (assuming that there is one) has been obscured.

One specific source of obscurity in titles is noun plague—the jamming together of nouns so that some function as adjectives:

The Texas Probable Future Competition Cases and the Transformation of the Bank Expansion Movement, 24 Antitrust Bull. 395 (1989).

The authors give us two long noun phrases joined by *and* in such a way that we have no clue about the relationship between the two. Are we to learn about the effect of the cases on the movement to expand banks, or vice versa? Can we have no hint of the proffered thesis, of the authors' views? This abstract blandness all but ensures that an article will go unread.

The opposite of noun plague is the stringing together of prepositional phrases, so these little relational words seem to take over:

The Use and Misuse of the Term "Consumer Welfare": Once More to the Mat on the Issue of Single Entity Status for Sports Leagues Under Section 1 of the Sherman Act, 64 Tul. L. Rev. 71 (1989).

The Sensitivity of Tests of the Intertemporal Allocation of Consumption to Near-Rational Alternatives, 79 Am. Econ. Rev. 319 (1989).

If you read those titles aloud a couple of times, you'll find yourself accenting the prepositions more than the other words.

Finally, in titles, as in other types of prose, undue alliteration can easily turn repulsive:

Preconfirmation or Preclosing Payment of Prepetition Claims in Bankruptcy, 94 Com. L.J. 187 (1989).[2]

To avoid this type of injudicious jingling (two in a row might be all right), keep your mind's ear alert as you're writing.

The chief virtues in titling are to be brief, apt, and evocative. Sanford Levinson's *Constitutional Faith* (1988) has each of these virtues. The title is indisputably brief. Beyond that, it is apt and evocative because the book develops parallels between constitutionalism and religion. The title economically suggests the comparison.

But don't feel impelled to evoke and suggest. Often, especially with a book, a brief descriptive phrase provides the best title. Take Oliver Wendell Holmes's masterpiece, *The Common Law*, or H.L.A. Hart and Tony Honoré's *Causation in the Law*, or Charles Alan Wright's classic hornbook, *The Law of Federal Courts*. These titles don't pretend to be witty. Yet in their brevity they capture the soul of wit.

4.2   Headings

Artfully employed, headings and subheadings make your writing easier to follow. They also help you, as a writer, keep your bearings. But keep three things in mind:

1. Don't rely solely on headings to provide transitions. You'll still need to prepare the reader—perhaps with a transitional word (*therefore*) or sentence (*That brings us to the final point*).
2. Be sure that any headings you use convey a definite message to the reader. A vague or ambiguous heading defeats itself.
3. Shun generic headings, such as "Facts" or "Background," "Analysis," and "Conclusion." These often falsely suggest that the facts are discrete from the analysis, or that the analysis is discrete from the conclusion. Unless you are writing in a medium that requires formulaic headings, such as the "Statement of Facts" in a brief or

---

2. For other examples of undesirable (as well as desirable) alliteration, see 6.15.

student memorandum, such headings give the impression that the writing follows a formula. And you may even make it formulaic by failing to analyze what organization best suits your purposes. Make your headings serve your text, not vice versa.

Two final notes. First, keep your headings fairly uniform in length—as brief as possible to get the message across. Some legal writers mar their prose by making the first heading 5 words long, the next one 40, the next one 20, and so on. Second, be consistent in using either complete sentences or just phrases in parallel headings.

4.3   Italics

'Tis a good rule of rhetoric which Schlegel gives,—"In good prose, every word is underscored," which, I suppose, means, Never italicize.
Ralph Waldo Emerson[3]

Italic type is the equivalent of underlining. But stick to one or the other in a single piece of writing. Formerly unavailable in the days of typewriters, italic type generally implies care in production. It puts less strain on the readers' eyes than underscored text does. Generally, if italic print is available, you should prefer it to underlining.

Italicizing your own words for emphasis is a typographic trick that can annoy readers. It implies that they need special help to follow your reasoning. Advocates sometimes emphasize every word, longish phrase, or even sentence that they would like the judge to read with special attention. They might as well forget the italics and instead use exclamation marks. *The comic effect is not so very different!* Instead of relying on typography to do the job for you, organize your words so that the emphasis naturally falls where you want it.

When you're quoting somebody else, you may need to use italics

---

3. *Lectures and Biographical Sketches*, in 10 COMPLETE WORKS OF EMERSON 169 (1904).

to be sure that readers don't overlook a key word or phrase. Even here, though, italicize sparingly.

Apart from emphasis, italics are used for (1) names of works, such as books and (in law) articles; (2) foreign words (*mano a mano, joie de vivre*); and (3) words used not for inherent meaning but as words (the word *legaldegook*).

4.4 Numbers

When science and mathematics aren't involved, the best practice is to spell out numbers, cardinal and ordinal, smaller than 11. (Another common practice is to spell out all numbers smaller than 101. Although this more formal practice is perfectly acceptable in legal writing, it can hamper readability.)

Not this:	*But this:*
Last year, ninety-two trials in the federal courts in this region consumed twenty days or more; the two longest trials lasted more than three months.	Last year, 92 trials in the federal courts in this region consumed 20 days or more; the 2 longest trials lasted more than three months.

There are six exceptions to the general principle:

1. If numbers recur throughout the text or are being used for calculations—that is, if the context is quasi-mathematical—then use numerals even for numbers smaller than 11.
2. Approximations are spelled out (*about three hundred years ago*).
3. In units of measure, words substitute for rows of zeros where possible (*$3 million, $3 billion*), and numerals are used with words of measure (*9 inches, 4 millimeters*).
4. Numbers that begin sentences must always be spelled out (*Two thousand was an auspicious year . . .*). But it's often better to reword the sentence so that it won't begin with a number.
5. Percentages may be written as numerals (*8%, 8 percent*) or spelled out (*eight percent*), but the first is preferable since it's more economical. And you're typically better off using the percentage sign: it conveys your meaning more lightly and quickly.

6. If, in the same context, some numbers are above the cutoff and
    some below in reference to the same types of things, use numer-
    als for all. Hence, in the example on page 79, 2 appears as a nu-
    meral and three is written out. And, for another example:

Not this:	*But this:*
Of the 160 Criminal Rules, only	Of the 160 Criminal Rules, only 3
three are to be amended.	are to be amended.

Some numbers require punctuation; others don't. Commas separate numerals into thousands (10,000), even when the number is
1,000. Square dollar amounts should not include zeros to indicate
cents: write $4,700, not $4,700.00. When referring to decades, omit
the apostrophe: hence, 1960s instead of 1960's. Finally, despite the
legal writer's habit, you need not, and should not, duplicate written amounts with numerals in parentheses: *six hundred (600) bales
of hay;* write simply *600 bales of hay.* For other puzzles with numbers, consult *The Chicago Manual of Style* (14th ed. 1993) or *Words
into Type* (3d ed. 1974).

4.5   Defined Terms

Many legal writers have become enamored of defined terms. Here,
as with footnotes, writers commonly mistake the forms of scholar-
ship for its substance. Although it may be convenient, even desirable, to refer to "the Agreement" and to know precisely what is
referred to, the habit has so insidiously worked its way into legal
writing that we sometimes see defined terms that are defined and
then never again used.

A certain judicial opinion defines the following terms: NYME,
FCM, EFP, REDCO, and TOI. Before we know it, we read that an
FCM represents REDCO before NYME, but that the FCM also has
duties to TOI, under EFP-1, to certify that TOI owned enough oil to
cover its EFP obligations. What ought to be a reader's shortcut has
become a writer's shortcut that obstructs the reader. Don't abuse
defined terms by cluttering the text with initialisms in this way.

Three points about midsentence definitions. First, use them sparingly—mostly for shorthand names of parties that might otherwise get confused with other people or organizations. Second, don't formally define when the meaning is clear from context. There's no reason to write *former Secretary of State Madeleine Albright ("Ms. Albright")* if there's only one Albright involved in the discussion. Third, never include legalisms such as *hereinafter referred to as*; the parentheses (with quotation marks inside) are enough to signal that it's a defined term. For more on avoiding pedantry in introducing defined terms, see 7.4.

4.6 Contractions

You might well have heard that contractions don't belong in legal writing. The view seems to be that they aren't professional. But that's just a shibboleth.

In fact, the decision whether to use a contraction often boils down to this: do I want to sound natural, or do I want to sound stuffy? A relaxed, confident writer who wants to sound unforced will need some contractions, as these examples illustrate:

Not this:	*But this:*
If a witness is unwilling to answer questions properly posed by an officer of the court, is it not likely that this is because the witness has something to hide?	If a witness is unwilling to answer questions properly posed by an officer of the court, isn't it likely that this is because the witness has something to hide?
The bailee would have been able to sue the thief. But probably that was not worth very much.	The bailee would have been able to sue the thief. But probably that wasn't worth very much.
Because the plaintiff has not pleaded with specificity, and now claims that he cannot do so, he should explain to the court why he cannot.	Because the plaintiff hasn't pleaded with specificity, and now claims that he can't do so, he should explain to the court why he can't.

Here's the test for when to use a contraction: whenever you'd ordinarily say it as a contraction, then write it that way.

Here's a great example from Michigan Judge J. H. Gillis, whose three-sentence opinion in *Denny v. Radar Industries, Inc.*[4] reads in full: "The appellant has attempted to distinguish the factual situation in this case from that in *Renfroe v. Higgins Rack Coating & Mfg. Co.* (1969), 17 Mich. App. 259, 169 N.W.2d 326. He didn't. We couldn't. Affirmed."

4.7   First Person

Shun phrases such as *the present writer, this writer,* and other such circumlocutions for the first person. These are useful devices for students of Freshman English, who often need weaning from constant reference to themselves (*I feel, I believe, in my opinion, it seems to me*). Having been weaned, however, you may adopt a natural style that doesn't obscure the person wielding the pen.

In his preface to *Courts on Trial,* Jerome Frank confessed that he had long shunned the first-person pronoun, preferring *the writer* to *I* on the assumption that the indirect phrasing signified modesty. With age he became wiser and concluded: "To say *I* removes a false impression of a Jovian aloofness; it means no more than *I think* or *I happen now to believe;* the reader is thus put on his guard."[5]

Of one common self-obscuring device—*it is suggested that* or *it is proposed that*—Fred Rodell observed, "Whether the writers really suppose that such constructions clothe them in anonymity so that people cannot guess who is suggesting and who is proposing, I do not know."[6] We do know, however, that these passive-voice phrases make sentences read as if they had been "translated from the German by someone with a rather meager knowledge of English."[7]

---

4. 184 N.W.2d 289 (Mich. Ct. App. 1970).
5. Jerome Frank, Courts on Trial vii–viii (1949; repr. 1950).
6. Fred Rodell, *Goodbye to Law Reviews—Revisited,* 48 Va. L. Rev. 279, 280 (1962).
7. *Id.*

Although judges are perfectly justified in using the first person—*I* and *me* for a single judge, *we* and *us* for an appellate tribunal—advocates rarely find occasion to inject their personalities; to do so would be not just mistaken, but unprofessional. The personal views of counsel are irrelevant. Instead, the general practice is to make all references to the client—not *I contend*, but *Blanchard contends*. As Blanchard's counsel, you are subsumed in such references. But it is also quite acceptable to say *we contend* (that is, you and your client).

4.8 Enumerations

The best method for enumerating ideas is the straightforward *first, second*, and *third*.

> The material defenses are, first, that the city had no power to make an exclusive contract; second, that the contract for rental of hydrants created an aggregate indebtedness prohibited by the Constitution of the State; and, third, that the water works company had not kept its contract . . . .[8]

> As we have interpreted § 5, suits involving the section may be brought in at least three ways. First, of course, the State may institute a declaratory judgment action. Second, an individual may bring a suit for declaratory judgment and injunctive relief . . . . Third, the Attorney General may bring an injunctive action to prohibit the enforcement of a new regulation because of the State's failure to obtain approval under § 5.[9]

The forms *firstly, secondly*, and *thirdly* have an unnecessary syllable, and using *one, two*, and *three* is especially informal.

Numbers or letters prove just as serviceable as *first, second*, and

---

8. City of Columbus v. Mercantile Trust & Deposit Co., 218 U.S. 645, 650 (1910) (per Lurton, J.).
9. Allen v. State Bd. of Elections, 393 U.S. 544, 561 (1969) (per Warren, C.J.).

third when you enumerate items in a single sentence, without much development from one idea to the next:

> Notably in America, codification has suffered from a failure to distinguish two incompatible aims: (1) the procuring of simplicity and (2) the procuring of precision.[10]

> Folley Oil Company sought damages for (1) the shutdown of the well, (2) the removal of defective tubing, (3) the purchase and installation of replacement tubing, and (4) the lost profits resulting from loss of production.

> The court held that the veracity of hearsay statements is sufficiently dependable to be admitted against an accused when (a) the evidence falls within a firmly rooted hearsay exception, or (b) it contains such "particularized guarantees of truthfulness" that adversarial testing would be expected to add little to its reliability.

4.9   Quotations

Legal writers quote a great deal. Judges and advocates find themselves quoting precedents, business lawyers quote contractual language, and estate lawyers quote wills. But legal writers too often fail to weave the quoted matter neatly into their own prose. Handling quotations deftly is one of the most difficult skills to master.

Quotations are commonly introduced in one of four ways: with no punctuation before the quotation marks, with a comma preceding, with a colon preceding, or with a full stop followed by a quoted sentence:

> To Chief Justice Chase, habeas corpus was the "best and only sufficient defence of personal freedom."

> As one of the foremost American jurists has written, "The most controversial and friction-producing issue in the relation between the federal courts and the states is federal habeas corpus for state prisoners."

---

10. Jerome Frank, Law and the Modern Mind 336 (1930; repr. 1963).

Professor Jenks announced a startling discovery: "The writ of habeas corpus was originally intended not to get people out of prison, but to put them in it."

Lord Chief Justice Cockburn took the opposite view of the question. "I deeply deplore that members of the Bar so frequently unnecessarily put questions affecting the private life of witnesses, which are only justifiable when they challenge the credibility of a witness."[11]

With block quotations, usually more than four lines or 50 words long, the rules are the same, even with the first of the preceding options. Hence (one writer quoting another):

Professor Bobbitt thinks that the view that moral arguments should generally be excluded from constitutional discourse

> justifies, for example, the phenomenon of federal habeas corpus, for which it is otherwise difficult to give good grounds. Habeas corpus severs the constitutional decision from the moral question of guilt or innocence, so that the former can be dispassionately weighed as one suspects it seldom can be in the context of a trial. At the same time federal habeas corpus gives the matter to a group of deciders whose customary business is, by comparison to state courts, largely amoral.[12]

Keep your quotations as trim as possible. Make them always germane. Use block quotations only as a last resort. Though you may be tempted to quote large chunks of others' writing to win your points, you drastically diminish the chances of having the material actually read. If you can't say what you mean in your own words, how well can others say it for you?

Unheralded shifts in voice, as from third person to first person within a single sentence, are a common fault in quoting.

---

11. Francis L. Wellman, The Art of Cross-Examination 201 (4th ed. 1936; repr. 1970) (last quotation only).
12. Philip Bobbitt, Constitutional Fate 140 (1982) (as quoted by another writer).

Not this:

In denying the motion for summary judgment, Judge Fitzwater stated that "I believe there exists an issue of material fact on the question of intent."

But this:

In denying the motion for summary judgment, Judge Fitzwater stated that he believed "there exists an issue of material fact on the question of intent."

Contrast the shifting voice in the first version with Wellman's quotation of Lord Chief Justice Cockburn on p. 85, where the first sentence adequately alerts the reader to the coming shift when Cockburn himself speaks (as opposed to the quoter).

Settled conventions determine how to punctuate the ends of quotations. In American English, commas and periods go inside the last quotation mark, but colons and semicolons go outside.

> He objected to being called a "ratcatcher," preferring instead the title "rodent operative."

> He objected to being called a "ratcatcher"; instead, he liked the title "rodent operative": it made him feel more dignified.

The placement of a question mark depends on whether the question is that of the writer or of the person quoted:

> Then she asked, "What is your name?"

> Did the police officer really say, "You're under arrest"?

4.10 Alterations and Ellipses

Although writers outside law sometimes tacitly change capitalization (and occasionally even punctuation) in quotations, the legal culture doesn't accept unmarked changes. We note every change in source materials. If you extract another's phrase and then uppercase the first word to begin your sentence, signal the change by putting the newly uppercased letter in square brackets: "[J]udges in the 17th century...." (The original source said: "It can hardly be gainsaid, then, that judges in the 17th century....") The principle applies also to lowercasing what had been an uppercased word in the quoted sentence. This punctilio, verging on pedantry, can be a virtue; in the legal writer, always needful of credibility, it has become a necessity.

As in the unfinished sentence in the previous paragraph, omission of one or more words in midsentence, or at the end of a sentence, is shown by a series of three dots (not asterisks) called ellipsis points. When the sentence ends with quoted material, use a fourth dot to end the sentence:

> It is difficult in a concurring judgment to say that you agree with most of what has been said. I agreed with the result . . . .[13]

But when you resume a sentence, with either your own words or quoted words, indicate the omission of words by using the three-point ellipsis:

> No one really doubts that the common law . . . develops . . . in response to the developments of the society in which it rules.[14]

When your ellipsis takes you into another sentence within the quotation, use four points to show that you have cut short the earlier sentence and omitted something. That something might be merely a phrase before or after the end of the sentence, or it might be several sentences long.

> I used to mention, very briefly, the two things [that] I thought lawyers should most particularly keep in mind. The first is to eliminate this continual cussing out of the lawyer on the other side. One hardly ever goes through the argument of a motion or the trial of a case without a number of these nasty recriminations. As far as I can tell, they never help the lawyer who makes them . . . . The other point . . . is that the lawyer must never forget that he is part of the admin-

---

13. Wright v. Walford [1955] 1 Q.B. 363, 367 (per Birkett, L.J.).
14. Lister v. Romford Ice & Cold Storage Co. [1957] A.C. 555, 591 (Lord Radcliffe, dissenting).

istration of justice and that it is his duty at all times to help the court.[15]

We don't know precisely how much material has been omitted where the first ellipsis appears. (In fact, half a sentence has been dropped.) We assume that the second ellipsis stands for only a brief omission because the sentence continues and makes perfect sense. (The words *I made* have dropped out.)

To indicate an omission of one or more paragraphs in a block quotation, devote a whole line to the three periods, and space them apart:

> The Court's inability to agree left its decisions weak and unpersuasive, and it came under wider attack.
>
> . . .
>
> Brandeis's presence on the Court, as Holmes had feared, put added strain on the relations among the justices, and added to the heat of public criticism. That tall, gaunt figure with deeply shadowed eyes, utterly unlike Taft, seemed to have every excess stripped away from him.[16]

The established practice in law is to omit ellipses at the beginning of any quotation, and before and after a quotation if the quoted passage is only a phrase or clause.[17] These omissions usually cause no difficulty. If the first word in the quoted material is lowercase, we know that the quotation begins in midsentence. If the first word is uppercase, we know that the beginning of the quotation is also the beginning of a sentence in the quoted material. If the first letter is bracketed, we know that the case has been changed from upper to lower, or vice versa.

> [N]ot all decisions, alas, are supported by clear and explicit rulings, though by the logic of formal justice there ought to be at least an im-

15. Harold R. Medina, *The Education of a Judge, in* THE ANATOMY OF FREEDOM 165, 169 (C. Waller Barrett ed., 1959).

16. SHELDON M. NOVICK, HONORABLE JUSTICE: THE LIFE OF OLIVER WENDELL HOLMES 343 (1989).

17. *See* THE BLUEBOOK § 5.3, at 46 (17th ed. 2000).

plicit ruling in any justifying opinion. [The beginning of the original sentence has been omitted.]

It appears on the face of it that the argument quoted has conclusive force; the learned judge certainly thought so, as appears from his expression of regret that "there must be judgment" against Mrs. Tarbard . . . .[18] [No ellipses before or after the internal quotation.]

As noted at the outset of this section, legal writers bracket interpolated words and letters. When brackets and ellipses proliferate, though, it's time to paraphrase, not quote and alter.

Not this:

These words seem to us, in Judge Learned Hand's memorable phrase, to "dance before [our] eyes in a meaningless procession . . . leav[ing] in [our] mind[s] only a confused sense of some vitally important, but successfully concealed purport."[19]

But this:

To paraphrase Judge Learned Hand's memorable statement, these words dance before our eyes in a meaningless procession, leaving in our minds only a confused sense of some crucial meaning.

4.11 Citations

Most readers have probably come across lawyers or law students who believe that legal style is primarily a matter of getting the citations right. "Stylists" of that stripe will be disappointed to find these paltry paragraphs on the subject; but these paltry paragraphs accord citations their due.

We are fortunate in the United States to have two good manuals: *The Bluebook*[20] and the *ALWD Citation Manual.*[21] In Great Britain, because there is no real equivalent, citing cases is less easy. (The

---

18. NEIL MACCORMICK, LEGAL REASONING AND LEGAL THEORY 21 (1978).
19. Kohler v. Tugwell, 292 F. Supp. 978, 980 n.9 (E.D. La. 1968) (brackets and ellipsis in original) (quoting Learned Hand, *Thomas Walter Swan, in* THE SPIRIT OF LIBERTY 209, 213 (Irving Dilliard ed., 2d ed. 1953)).
20. THE BLUEBOOK (17th ed. 2000).
21. ALWD CITATION MANUAL (2000).

American rules for British citations don't follow established British conventions.) Although Chicago's *Maroonbook*[22] has its few attractions, allowing discretionary forms of citation, as it does, would cause inconsistencies to proliferate: the librarian's and cite-checker's nightmare.

Many *Bluebook* rulemongers forget what was once—and still should be—the *Bluebook's* most important statement: the *Bluebook's* commands are to be cheerfully abandoned "when unusual circumstances make [the prescribed] forms confusing or otherwise inadequate."[23] Unfortunately, the past three editions have dropped the statement.

One point merits close attention: place citations so as to have them available but out of the way. Always subordinate citations to the statements they support. Never begin a sentence with a citation. By the time your readers get to the first parallel citation in the second line of your "sentence" and realize that no thoughts have yet filtered through, they will decide that you're a writer who deserves, at the very most, a quick scan.

Midsentence citations are equally interruptive, sometimes outright disruptive. They may even be comical:

> The doctrine of incorporation by reference, even if applicable at all where an intent to incorporate in the usual sense is negatived (*In re Estate of York*, 95 N.H. 435, 437, 65 A.2d 282, 8 A.L.R.2d 611; Lauritzen, *Can a Revocable Trust Be Incorporated by Reference?*, 45 Ill. L. Rev. 583, 600; Polasky, *"Pourover" Wills and the Statutory Blessing*, 98 Trusts & Estates 949, 954–955; compare *Old Colony Trust Co. v. Cleveland*, 921 Mass. 380, 196 N.E. 920; *Bolles v. Toledo Trust Co.*, 144 Ohio St. 195, 58 N.E.2d 381, 157 A.L.R. 1164; Restatement [2d]: Trusts, § 54, comments e–j, l), could not import the nonexistent amendment.[24]

---

22. THE UNIVERSITY OF CHICAGO MANUAL OF LEGAL CITATION (1989).
23. A UNIFORM SYSTEM OF CITATION iv (14th ed. 1986).
24. Second Bank-State St. Trust Co. v. Pinion, 170 N.E.2d 350, 352 (Mass. 1960).

Do those parentheses really make the reader's toil any easier?

Only when the citation is necessary and unobtrusive ought the citation to go in midsentence:

> Our holding in *Harrington v. Bush*, 553 F.2d 190 (D.C. Cir. 1977), requires us to reject Senator Helms's arguments and to deny him standing.[25]

If not at the beginning and not in the middle of a sentence, then where should you generally put citations? Bring the sentence to an end and put the citation after.

Or you might do something else: put your citations in footnotes whenever possible. But do this in such a way that your readers won't have to glance constantly to the foot of the page: say what your authority is in the text, and put the bibliographic information in footnotes. For example:

Not this:	*But this:*
The effect of a release is to extinguish any claim that a plaintiff might otherwise have against a defendant. *Pellett v. Sonotone Corp.*, 26 Cal. 2d 705, 711, 160 P.2d 783, 786 (1945). Indeed, when a release employs absolute terms, as here, there can be no question about its effect. *See Winet v. Price*, 4 Cal. App. 4th 1159, 1166, 6 Cal. Rptr. 2d 554 (1992) (holding that a plaintiff's claim was barred by a release wherein "the parties declared their intention to release each other from all claims, known or unknown, suspected or unsus-	The effect of a release is to extinguish any claim that a plaintiff might otherwise have against a defendant. The California Supreme Court so held in *Pellett v. Sonotone Corp.*, the leading case, decided in 1945.[1] Intermediate courts have consistently followed *Pellett*, especially when the release employs absolute terms, as it does here. Two recent cases from this Court are directly on point. In the 1992 case of *Winet v. Price*,[2] the Court held that a plaintiff's claim was barred by a release from "all claims, known or unknown, suspected or unsuspected, arising

---

25. Southern Christian Leadership Conf. v. Kelley, 747 F.2d 777, 780 (D.C. Cir. 1984).

pected, arising from . . . the facts described in the underlying lawsuit," despite the plaintiff's contention that it was not his subjective intent to release a right to sue in the future); *San Diego Hospice v. County of San Diego*, 31 Cal. App. 4th 1048, 1053, 37 Cal. Rptr. 2d 501 (1995) (explaining that "a general release can be completely enforceable and act as a complete bar to all claims known or unknown at the time of the release, despite protestations by one of the parties that he did not intend to release certain types of claims").

from . . . the facts described in the underlying lawsuit."[3] Although the plaintiff contended that he did not subjectively intend to release a right to sue in the future, the Court found the argument unpersuasive.[4] And three years later, in *San Diego Hospice v. County of San Diego*,[5] the Court reaffirmed this principle, stating that "a general release can be completely enforceable and act as a complete bar to all claims known or unknown at the time of the release, despite protestations by one of the parties that he did not intend to release certain types of claims."

The superscripts in the right-hand column merely take the reader to the volumes and pages where the cases can be found.

This technique has many advantages. The chief ones are that (1) you have to discuss the caselaw contextually, without reducing holdings into parentheticals; (2) you can more easily vary the length and structure of your sentences; and (3) you'll be writing sharper paragraphs (often shorter paragraphs) that contain more information in actual prose.

4.12 Footnotes

It is a measure of the legal distemper that we see news articles, from time to time, about the record for the number of footnotes in a law-review piece. At last count, the record had approached 5,000 footnotes in a single article. We have enough difficulty wading through an article 5,000 words long; quadruple the length of the article, add in several thousand footnotes, and you overwhelm even the most intrepid reader. Slogging through your "telephone book" will prove almost as taxing as climbing Mount Everest, which at least carries with it some glory.

Numerosity is one thing. Purpose is another. If you use footnotes to say "On the other hand" at every turn, you create flabby prose. If you develop every byway of the argument in substantive footnotes—that is, footnotes that contain further discussion of an issue—you diffuse the analysis. If a point merits lengthy development, then develop it in the text, not in the netherworld of footnotes.

Outlawing footnotes would oppress the responsible users. Still, we must dispel the canard that "[e]very legal writer is presumed to be a liar until he proves himself otherwise with a flock of footnotes."[26] The irony of that tongue-in-cheek statement, by Fred Rodell, is that our best legal writers footnote lightly. Indeed, Rodell himself wrote *Nine Men*, a political history of the United States Supreme Court, using neither footnotes nor citations. Although these omissions occasionally prove inconvenient, readers can appreciate the liberated page.

Footnotes sometimes prove invaluable, as in a treatise that gives holdings, jurisdiction by jurisdiction, on a particular point of law. Such a treatise is intended as a reference work, not as a book to be read from cover to cover. The footnotes lead you to the cases you need in research. But even when gratefully consulting such a work, you can hardly ignore, at the foot of every page, the notes that "run along, like little angry dogs barking at the text."[27] These days, the notes are more likely Great Danes than chihuahuas.

As in all matters of writing, judgment and discretion control—not absolute prescriptions or proscriptions. If you scrupulously avoid footnotes, you'll win over more readers than if you make a fetish of them. Setting a footnote record is a cause more for embar-

26. Fred Rodell, *Goodbye to Law Reviews—Revisited*, 48 VA. L. REV. 279, 282 (1962).
27. Samuel M. Crothers, *That History Should Be Readable, in* THE GENTLE READER 172 (1903; repr. 1972).

rassment than for pride, even if you find your record celebrated in the *Wall Street Journal.*[28]

4.13 Forms of Address and Reference

To avoid professional blunders in correspondence and other writings, the legal writer needs to know how to refer to judges and other dignitaries. The American rules are much simpler than the British ones. Only a few of the most basic questions are treated here. For a fuller discussion, consult one of the several books in print on forms of address,[29] or a good book of etiquette. Do your homework.

In addressing judges, err on the side of formality, but not to the point of archaism or pedantry.

Not this:	*But this:*
To the Honorable Judge of Said Court:	To the Honorable Court:
	or:
	To the Honorable Alicemarie H. Stotler, District Judge:

In corresponding with the federal judiciary, follow these forms:

Chief Justice
    (very formal) The Chief Justice of the United States[30]
    (address)
        Dear Mr. Chief Justice:

---

28. *See* Paul Barrett, *To Read This Story in Full, Don't Forget to See the Footnotes,* WALL ST. J., 10 May 1988, at 1.
29. *See, e.g.,* PATRICK MONTAGUE-SMITH, DEBRETT'S CORRECT FORM (1st rev. ed. 1976; repr. 1989); TITLES AND FORMS OF ADDRESS (18th ed. 1985); HOWARD MEASURES, STYLES OF ADDRESS: A MANUAL OF USAGE IN WRITING AND SPEECH (rev. ed. 1962).
30. Note the correct title: not *Chief Justice of the Supreme Court of the United States,* but *Chief Justice of the United States.*

(less formal) The Honorable William H. Rehnquist
The Chief Justice of the United States
(address)
    Dear Chief Justice Rehnquist:

Associate Justice
The Honorable Ruth Bader Ginsburg
The Supreme Court of the United States
(address)
    Dear Justice Ginsburg:

Other federal judge
The Honorable (full name)
(name of court)
(local address)
    Dear Judge (surname):

In corresponding with state judges, follow these forms (applicable in most states):

Chief Justice of highest appellate tribunal
The Honorable (full name)
Chief Justice, (name of court)
(local address)
    Dear Chief Justice (surname):

Other state judge
The Honorable (full name)
(name of court)
(local address)
    Dear Judge (surname):[31]

Four caveats will save you from dishonor. First, *Honorable* should be capitalized whenever coupled with a person's name. Sec-

---

31. In some states, intermediate appellate judges or even trial judges (of general jurisdiction) are given the title "justice." Where that is so, use the title "justice" in both the address and the salutation.

ond, never write "The Honorable O'Connor" or "Hon. O'Connor." *Honorable* always takes a full name. Third, abbreviate *Honorable* only in addresses, and omit *The* when abbreviating. Fourth, when writing to a British, Canadian, or Australian correspondent and spelling out the word, use the British spelling:

> The Right Honourable the Lord Woolf of Barnes

Except in historical contexts, avoid labels that readers may find gratuitously sexist, such as

> Mr. Justice Souter
>
> Madam Justice O'Connor
>
> Mrs. Justice Ginsburg

Though the *Mr.* is needed in the formal salutation *Dear Mr. Chief Justice*, many American lawyers and judges consider the three forms just listed offensive. In Great Britain, they are considered less offensive; indeed, to many they are fully acceptable. Know your audience.

Referring to judges in the third person has its complications. Whereas British legal writers tend to refer in discourse to

> Denning M.R.

and

> Woolf L.J.

without even a comma after the name, Americans generally refer to

> Chief Justice Rehnquist

and

> Judge Robert E. Keeton (on first mention; then Judge Keeton).

In third-person contexts, avoid honorifics such as *The Honorable*.

How should lawyers refer to one another? The American practice of appending *Esq.* to others' names is entirely acceptable, but no other titles (not even *Mr.*) may be used in conjunction with it (see pp. 113–14). If you prefer not to use *Esq.* (some consider it clubby or pretentious), a mere *Mr.* or *Ms.* or *Mrs.* (or even *Miss*, depending on the addressee's preference) will always suffice. British lawyers often have titles or affiliations that a correspondent is obliged to include after the addressee's name, such as *Q.C.* (Queen's Counsel) and *F.B.A.* (Fellow of the British Academy).

4.14 Signing Off

Whether in court papers or in letters, dispense with the archaic flourishes.

Not this:	*But this:*
Pleading	
Wherefore, premises considered, plaintiff respectfully prays that	Johnson respectfully requests that . . . .
Letter	
I remain, my dear sir,	Sincerely yours,
Sincerely yours,	

In business and personal letters, you may show some individuality in the complimentary close by adopting any of the several standard forms:

Very formal and deferential
    Respectfully (yours),
    Very respectfully (yours),

Less formal, without deference (as in demand letters)
    Very truly yours,
    Yours very truly,
    Yours truly,

General
    Sincerely (yours),
    Yours sincerely,

Informal
    With best wishes,
    Best wishes,
    With best regards,
    Best regards,
    Kindest personal regards,

Intimate
    As ever,
    Fondly,
    Yours,
    Yours ever (or always),

A foul rumor is afoot in the American legal profession that it is an error to close with *Sincerely, Respectfully, Fondly,* or any other adverb without adding *yours.* Don't believe it: every modern complimentary close has unexpressed, understood words within it. Respected writers from Supreme Court justices to preeminent law professors, even great poets, use *Sincerely* without saying whose.[32]

Finally, avoid ending with participial clauses in the final sentence.

Not this:	*But this:*

Hoping that we can move toward an early resolution of this matter, (I am)
    Very truly yours,
	I hope that we can soon resolve this matter.
	    Very truly yours,

Trusting that you will hold these matters in confidence,
    Yours sincerely,
	I trust that you will hold these matters in confidence.
	    Sincerely yours,

---

32. Charles Alan Wright, Bryan A. Garner & James D. Maugans, *The Wright–Garner–Maugans Correspondence on Complimentary Closes,* 2 SCRIBES J. LEGAL WRITING 83–99 (1991).

FIVE

Words and Expressions Confused and Misused

Exactness in the use of words is the basis of all serious thinking.
You will get nowhere without it. Words are clumsy tools,
and it is very easy to cut one's fingers with them, and they need
the closest attention in handling; but they are the only tools we have,
and imagination itself cannot work without them.
—*J.W. Allen*[1]

The English language teems with troublesome words. They prove just as troublesome for lawyers as for other writers. So a catalogue of words that lawyers regularly cut their fingers on must include many terms that aren't specifically legal. What follows is a sketch of English usage for the legal writer.

For a full treatment of usage—including a more extensive analysis of nuances of the rules and the reasons for the judgments here set forth—see my *Dictionary of Modern Legal Usage* (2d ed. 1995) and *Dictionary of Modern American Usage* (1998). Many other books will help you resolve questions about the most appropriate uses of English words. Every self-respecting writer ought to own an unabridged dictionary: *Webster's Third New International Dic-*

---

1. *Essay on Jeremy Bentham, in* THE SOCIAL AND POLITICAL IDEAS OF THE REVOLUTIONARY ERA 181, 199 (F.J.C. Hearnshaw ed., 1931) (describing the "essence of Bentham's teaching").

tionary (1961), *The Random House Dictionary of the English Language* (2d ed. 1987), or the *Oxford English Dictionary* (2d ed. 1989). American collegiate dictionaries provide ready reference: *Webster's Tenth New Collegiate Dictionary* (1993), *Webster's New World Dictionary* (4th ed. 1999), *Random House Webster's College Dictionary* (2d ed. 1997), and *The American Heritage Dictionary of the English Language* (4th ed. 2000).

a; an. *A* is used before words beginning with a consonant sound, including -*y*- and -*w*- sounds. *An* is used before words beginning with a vowel sound.

> a European country

> a historian

> an LL.B. degree

> an SEC subpoena

> a uniform

above-mentioned, above-listed, before-mentioned, etc. Simplify these cumbersome phrases.

Poor
> the above-mentioned court

Better
> the court (or give the name of the court again)

absolve (of) (from). One is *absolved of* financial liability and *absolved from* wrongdoing—assuming that the courts treat one kindly.

accommodation. So spelled. *Accomodation* is a common misspelling.

acknowledgment. So spelled in American English. The British usually write *acknowledgement,* with an extra -*e*-. Cf. **judgment.**

adapt; adopt. To *adapt* something is to modify it for one's own purposes. To *adopt* something is to accept it wholesale and use it.

admittance; admission. The first is purely physical <No admittance>, whereas the second is used mostly in figurative and non-physical senses <admission to the bar>. *Admission* is also used, however, in physical senses when rights or privileges are attached to gaining entry: "The *admission* of aliens into the United States is more restricted today than it was in the past."

adverse; averse. To be *adverse* to something is to be turned in opposition against it; to be *averse* to something is to have feelings against it. We usually think of circumstances as being *adverse* and of people as being *averse* to something. But in law, with our adversary system, we often refer to *adverse parties*.

adviser; advisor. Use the -*er* spelling. Note, however, that the adjective is spelled *advisory*.

affect; effect. Ordinarily, *affect* (= to influence) is a verb, and *effect* (= a result or consequence) is a noun. But *effect* is also, less commonly, a verb meaning "to bring about, produce." See **effect**.

aforementioned; aforesaid. Expunge these lawyerisms; they have little or no justification in modern writing.

aggravate. Avoid this word in place of *annoy* or *irritate*. In formal prose, *aggravate* (literally "to add weight to") means "to make worse, exacerbate."

alibi. This is a specific legal term referring to the defense of having been at a place other than the scene of a crime. The word should not apply to just any excuse or explanation for misconduct.

all . . . not. *Not all* is usually the correct sequence in negative constructions.

Poor
   All writers did not accept Lord Coke's dictum.

Better
> Not all writers accepted Lord Coke's dictum.

all of. Omit *of* <all the depositions>, except when the following word is a pronoun <all of us were deposed> or a possessive noun <all of Smith's many motions>.

all ready; already. The first has to do with preparation <we are all ready>, the second with time <we're finished already>.

all together. See **altogether.**

allude; elude. To *allude* is to refer to something indirectly or by suggestion only.

> In closing argument, the lawyer improperly alluded to the defendant's prior convictions.

To *elude* is to avoid or escape.

> The escaped prisoner eluded police for three days.

allusion; illusion. The first is an indirect reference <literary allusion>, the second a deception <optical illusion>.

already. See **all ready.**

alternative; alternate. An *alternative* is a choice or option—usually one of two choices, but not necessarily. An *alternate* is either something that proceeds by turns with another or a person who substitutes for another.

altogether; all together. The first means "completely, wholly," or "in all."

> The claims were not altogether unfounded. [They weren't wholly unfounded.]

> Altogether, 4,000 members attended the bar convention. [There were 4,000 in all.]

The second means "at one place or at the same time" <the defendants were tried all together>.

amend; emend. The first means "to put right" or "to add to"; the second means "to correct (as a text)." The nouns are *amendment* and *emendation*.

among; between. The oversimple formula is to say that *between* goes with two things and *among* with more than two. But don't refer to the space "among" three points. The true distinction is that *between* expresses one-to-one relations of two or more things, while *among* expresses collective and undefined relations of three or more things.

Negotiations continued between the various nations.

That belief is widely held among board members.

and/or. Banish from your working vocabulary this "much condemned conjunctive-disjunctive crutch of sloppy thinkers."[2]

Poor

    a fine of $25 and/or imprisonment for not more than 30 days

Better

    a fine of $25 or imprisonment for not more than 30 days, or both

The word *or* usually includes the sense of *and*:

No food or drink allowed.

That sentence does not suggest that food or drink by itself is disallowed while food and drink together are OK. See 2.12.

appraisal; appraisement. *Appraisal* is the preferred term in most contexts. *Appraisement* usually refers to the official valuation of estates.

appraise; apprize; apprise. The first two mean "to estimate the value of"; the second means, in addition, "to value highly"; the third means "to inform."

---

2. Raine v. Drasin, 621 S.W.2d 895, 905 (Ky. 1981).

She had the jewels appraised.

She apprized knowledge for its own sake.

Counsel apprised the judge of developments in the settlement talks.

apt. See **liable.**

arguendo. Unnecessary and (for many readers) obscure in place of *for the sake of argument.* In British legal contexts, *arguendo* usually means "during the course of argument"—so unless your readers are all Americans, the word may be ambiguous even to those familiar with it.

as. See **like.**

as far as . . . is concerned. Wordy filler.

Poor
> As far as any damages are concerned, we expect them to be insignificant.

Better
> We expect any damages to be insignificant.

One poor way to fix the poor phrasing is to drop *is concerned.* But those two words are idiomatically required if you begin with *as far as.*

as of yet. See **as yet.**

as per. Help stamp out this unrefined bit of legaldegook and commercialese. Use *in accordance with* or, if you insist on greater brevity, *per* alone.

assure; ensure; insure. A person *assures* (makes promises to, convinces) other persons and *ensures* (makes certain) that things happen. *Insure* should be restricted to financial contexts involving indemnification; it refers to what insurance companies do.

as to. Use this phrase only at the beginning of a sentence <As to the other plaintiffs, their claims are barred>. As a preposition, *as to* should always be replaced by a more specific word (*of, on, with, for, to, by, in, to, into*) or dropped completely, as here:

> The trial court failed to *specify as to what* [read *specify what*] the plaintiff relied on.

as yet. Like the variation *as of yet*, this phrase is invariably inferior to *yet* alone, *thus far*, or some other equivalent phrase.

a while; awhile. After a preposition, spell it as two words <He rested for a while>. But the adverbial use is usually more concise <He rested awhile>.

bad; badly. Write *I feel badly* if you have been anesthetized, but *I feel bad* when you are ill or regret something. If you have trouble keeping the two straight, analogize the choice to that between *I smell badly* and *I smell bad*: they mean completely different things.

basis, on a . . . . Generally, avoid this long-winded phrase.

Poor
>   The standard must be applied on a case-by-case basis.

Better
>   The standard must be applied case by case.

before-mentioned. See **above-mentioned; aforementioned.**

between. See **among.**

between you and I. A blunder for *between you and me*. See 2.22.

biannual; biennial. *Biannual*, like *semiannual*, means "occurring twice a year." *Biennial* means "occurring once every two years." But in other temporal instances, *bi-* means "every two" (*biweekly, bimonthly*) and stands in contrast with *semi-*, meaning "twice every" (*semiweekly, semimonthly*). So to eliminate confusion, write *twice-yearly* or *semiannual*, not *biannual*.

blame (on). In the best usage, you *blame* a person *for* something; you do not, properly, *blame* a thing *on* a person.

blatant; flagrant. What is *blatant* stands out glaringly or repugnantly. What is *flagrant* is deplorable and shocking, or "flaming," as Samuel Johnson defined it; the term connotes brazenness or outrage. A perjurer might tell *blatant* lies to a grand jury to cover up for his *flagrant* breach of trust.

can; may. Generally, *can* expresses physical or mental ability.

> He can lift 500 pounds.

May expresses permission or authorization, or possibility.

> *Permission:* The defense may now close.

> *Possibility:* The trial may end on Friday.

capital; capitol. The first is a city, the seat of government; the second is a building in which the state or national legislature meets.

case. This word best refers only to a legal case, a medical case, a grammatical case, or a case of wine. In legal writing, avoid such phrases as *in any case* (read *in any event*), *in case* (read *if*), *in every case* (read *always* or *in every instance*), *as is often the case* (read *often*), and *as the case may be* (reword the idea).

case of, in the. Instead of discussing a precedent by saying "In the case of *Brown v. Board of Education*," say simply "In *Brown v. Board of Education.*"

censor; censure. To *censor* is to scrutinize and revise, to suppress or edit selectively. To *censure* is to criticize severely, to castigate.

center around. Something can *center on* or *revolve around* something else, but it cannot *center around*, since the center is technically a single point.

certainly. See **obviously**.

character; reputation. *Character* is what one is, *reputation* what one is thought by others to be.

claim. This verb originally meant "to lay claim to," but it is now often used in the sense "to allege, assert."

> She claimed that the contract had been rescinded.

In this sense, *claim* often suggests an unsubstantiated assertion:

> McCandless claimed that the defendant ran a red light, but the evidence was against him.

Avoid using the word merely as a substitute for *say* or *state.*

As a noun, *claim* properly denotes either "a demand for something" <a patent claim> or "that which is demanded" <her claim was 40 acres>. Using the noun as an equivalent of *assertion* is now acceptable:

> The defendant cannot support his claim that the plaintiff's case is time-barred.

clearly. See **obviously.**

commence. Begin or start—do not commence.

common; mutual. *Common* means "shared by two or more."

> Despite their considerable differences, they found political common ground.

Mutual means "reciprocal, joint."

> Their affection was mutual.

One may have a friend or an interest *in common* with another. Avoid the phrases *mutual friend* (spoken, remember, by a Dickensian illiterate), *mutual interest* (unless affection is involved), and the like.

common(-)law. Hyphenate the phrase when it functions as an adjective <common-law misdemeanors>, but make it two words as a noun phrase <the common law forbade such evidence>. See 2.10.

compare (to) (with). *Compare with*, the usual phrase, means to place side by side, noting differences and similarities between the things compared. *Compare to* means to observe or point only to similarities.

compendium. An abridgment—not, as some mistakenly believe, a vast tome. *Compendious*, the adjective, means "abridged, shortened," not "voluminous."

comprise; compose. The parts *compose* the whole; the whole *comprises* the parts; the whole is *composed* of the parts; the parts are *comprised* in the whole. That is, the first ten constitutional amendments compose the Bill of Rights; the Bill of Rights comprises the first ten amendments. The phrase *is comprised of* is never correct.

conclusory. This term means "expressing a factual inference without stating the fundamental facts on which the inference is based." Because it is far more common in legal writing than its variants, *conclusional* and *conclusionary*, it is preferable to them.

congressional. Lowercased, unless part of a title or an organization's name. Cf. **constitutional**; **federal**.

consensus. So spelled. Avoid the redundant expressions *consensus of opinion* and *general consensus*.

consider (as). When followed by a noun or noun phrase, *consider as* is almost never justified—omit *as*.

Poor
> We considered him as a brilliant advocate.

Better
> We considered him a brilliant advocate.

The one exception occurs when *considered* means "examined" or "discussed."

> Holmes considered as a stylist

> Churchill considered as a historian

consist of; consist in. The phrase *consist of* refers to materials and precedes the physical elements that compose a tangible thing:

Cement *consists of* sand, gravel, and mortar.

Consist in, meaning "to have essence of," precedes abstract elements or qualities, or intangible things:

A good moral character *consists in* integrity, decency, fairness, and compassion.

constitutional. Lowercased thus. Cf. **congressional**; **federal**.

contemptible; contemptuous; contumacious. *Contemptible* means "worthy of contempt or scorn." *Contemptuous* and *contumacious* both mean roughly "scornful," but the latter is more frequently used as a legal term meaning "in contempt; willfully disobedient of a court order."

continual; continuous. The first means "frequently recurring, intermittent":

continual interruptions

continual complaints

The second means "occurring without interruption, unceasing":

a continuous flow of water

continuous possession

council; counsel. *Council* (= a deliberative assembly) is primarily a noun. *Counsel* (= to advise) is primarily a verb, but as a noun in legal writing it refers to "a legal adviser or advisers." Do not use the plural form *counsels.*

councilor; counselor. The first is one who serves on a council; the second is a lawyer or other adviser.

credible; creditable; credulous. *Credible* = believable. *Creditable* = worthy of credit, laudable. *Credulous* = gullible, tending to believe.

criterion. One *criterion*, two or more *criteria*.

culpability. See **guilt**.

damage; damages. *Damage* = loss or injury to person or property. *Damages* = monetary compensation for such a loss or injury.

deem. Often unnecessary, and usually stilted. Deem it to be undesirable in your writing—that is, avoid it.

defamation; libel; slander. *Defamation* = an attack on the reputation of another. It encompasses both *libel* (in permanent form, especially writing) and *slander* (in transitory form, especially spoken words).

demean. Authorities on usage formerly disapproved of *demean* in the sense "to lower, degrade," holding that instead it is properly reflexive and means "to conduct (oneself)." New lawyers often chuckle over the oath they must take (in one form or another):

> I pledge to *demean* myself as an officer of the court.

The more common lay sense, the one that gives rise to the double entendre, has been with us since at least 1601 and has become widespread in legal prose.

> This illogical result *demeans* the values protected by the Confrontation Clause.[3]

de minimis. So spelled. The phrase is commonly misrendered as if it ended in *-us*.

deprecate; depreciate. *Deprecate* = to disapprove regretfully.

> The judge deprecated the conduct of the defendant officers.

Depreciate = (1) to belittle <self-depreciating>, or (2) to fall in value <depreciating currency>. Today, however, the phrase *self-deprecating* (though it originated in error) is so common that it is standard American English.

---

3. Richardson v. Marsh, 481 U.S. 200, 212 (1987) (Stevens, J., dissenting).

different than. Generally, use *different from.*

> This case is markedly different from *Seven Elves.*

Doing so gives us a continuity with the verb form: *differs from*, not *differs than.*

Occasionally, however, when the phrase introduces a clause rather than a noun phrase, *different than* is not easily avoidable:

> Wakefield is a *different* person mentally and emotionally *than* he was before his loss of hearing.

In such a sentence, using *from what* instead of *than* would be awkward.

discrete; discreet. The first means "separate, distinct." The second means "cautious, judicious."

disinterested. Especially in legal writing, this word should be kept to its literal sense: "not having a personal interest and therefore impartial; free from bias." Don't misuse it for *uninterested* (= lacking interest). Judges should be disinterested in carrying out their responsibilities, but never uninterested.

disposal; disposition. Both mean "a getting rid of." But *disposal* more often has to do with trash or inconsequential things (or appears in the phrase *at one's disposal*), whereas *disposition* is used of a preconceived plan of orderly arrangement <disposition of assets> <disposition of a case>.

doubtless. This is the correct adverb; *doubtlessly* is wrong.

due to. This phrase means "attributable to" or "the result of" and should follow the verb *to be.* But the phrase is often used loosely in place of conjunctive adverbs meaning "as the result of": *because of, owing to, caused by,* or *on grounds of.*

> *Poor*
> She was late to court *due to* a traffic accident that delayed traffic in the downtown area.

Better

> She was late to court *because of* a traffic accident that delayed traffic in the downtown area.

> Her lateness to court was *due to* a traffic accident that delayed traffic in the downtown area. (This rewording is not as good because it's awkward.)

each and every. Discard this trite phrase.

each other; one another. The first is used of two persons or entities:

> The two men hated each other.

The second is best confined to contexts involving more than two:

> The three women respected one another.

-edly. Words ending in this way are more pervasive in law than elsewhere. Often the classic adverbial formula *in a . . . manner* does not work with such words—*allegedly* does not mean "in an alleged manner," *purportedly* does not mean "in a purported manner," and *admittedly* does not mean "in an admitted manner." Rather, the unorthodox formula for these words is passive: *it is ____ed that.* Thus, *allegedly* = it is alleged that, *concededly* = it is conceded that, *purportedly* = it is purported that. Instead of bewailing how unorthodox these words are, we should, without overworking them, be thankful for the terseness they make possible. Other such words include *supposedly, assertedly, reportedly,* and *confessedly.*

effect; effectuate. The emerging difference between these verbs is that *effect* means "to bring about or accomplish" <to effect a change in the law>, whereas *effectuate* means "to give effect to" <to effectuate the administration's stated policies>. See **affect.**

e.g.; i.e. The first, short for *exempli gratia,* means "for example."

> He tries all types of cases, e.g., commercial cases, personal-injury cases, divorces.

The second, short for *id est*, means "that is."

> She is dean of the law school, i.e., the final authority on matters of this kind.

Generally, as in the examples just given, these abbreviated phrases should be set off by commas.

either. See **nor** and 3.5 (pp. 71–73).

emend. See **amend.**

emigrate; immigrate. The first means "to migrate away from or exit (a country)." The second means "to migrate into or enter (a country)."

eminent. See **imminent.**

enclosed please find. The phrase is swollen deadwood in lawyers' correspondence. Write *I have enclosed* or (less good) *Enclosed is.*

enjoin. The word has opposite senses: (1) "to direct, mandate," and (2) "to prohibit." In sense 1, the verb takes the preposition *to* or *upon*:

> Secrecy is enjoined upon the jurors.

> We are enjoined to decide only actual cases or controversies.

In sense 2, the usual preposition is *from*:

> The court enjoined the pilots from continuing the strike.

enormity; enormousness. *Enormity* = outrageousness, hideousness. Don't use the word to denote size. *Enormousness* = hugeness, vastness.

ensure. See **assure.**

equally as . . . as. This wording is incorrect. *Equally as good as*, for example, wrongly displaces *as good as* or *equally good.*

Esq. This abbreviation is commonly used in the United States after the names of lawyers, men and women alike. The abbreviation is never to be put on one's own name—as on a business card or stationery. Nor should it be used with any other title, such as *Mr.* or *Ms.* In Great Britain, *esquire* is used of any man thought to have the social status of a gentleman. See pp. 96–97.

et al. See **etc.**

etc. Short for *et cetera* (= and other things). Lawyers should generally—in pleadings, for example—attempt to be as specific as possible instead of resorting to this term. Still, it would be foolish to lay down an absolute proscription against using *etc.* because often one cannot practicably list all that should be listed. Rather than convey to the reader that a list is seemingly complete when it is not, the writer can justifiably use *etc.* (always the abbreviation). Use the serial comma before this word (see 2.1), but don't include the word *and.* Be careful not to use *etc.* after a list of persons; *et al.,* short for *et alia* (= and others), serves that function. Cf. **inter alia.**

evidence. See **proof.**

evidentiary. This is the customary word, not *evidential.*

exceptionable; exceptional. The first is sometimes misused for the second. *Exceptionable* = open to exception; objectionable. *Exceptional* = out of the ordinary; uncommon; rare; superior.

fact. A fact cannot literally be false; if something is a fact, then it is by its very nature true. Yet in law we frequently use *facts* as a short form of *alleged facts:*

> No order may recite *untrue* facts.

Whenever possible, avoid that type of elliptical expression. Still, the tautology (*true facts*) and the oxymoron (*untrue facts*) are not likely to disappear from legal writing.

factor. The word properly means "an agent or cause that contributes to a particular result." Avoid using it in the slipshod sense "a thing to be considered; event; occurrence." See 7.17.

farther; further. The first refers to physical distances <farther than 250 yards>; the second, to figurative distances <extending the immunity even further>. The distinction likewise applies to *farthest* and *furthest*.

faze. See **phase.**

federal. Lowercased thus, unless part of a title or an organization's name. Cf. **congressional; constitutional.**

fewer. See **less.**

finalize. A favorite word of jargonmongers. For that reason alone, and also because the coinage does not fill a gap in the language (use *make final*), it is to be eschewed. See **-ize.**

first(ly), second(ly), third(ly). See 4.8.

flagrant. See **blatant.**

flaunt; flout. Don't flout the correct use of *flaunt*, which means "to show off or parade (something) in a flamboyant way" <"Marshall . . . flaunted to the nation the doctrine of judicial supremacy"— Fred Rodell>. *Flout* means "to contravene or disregard; to treat with contempt" <flouting the police officer's command>.

forbear; forebear. The first is a verb meaning "to tolerate; to refrain from objecting to." The second is a noun meaning "ancestor."

forbid. *Forbade* is the past tense, *forbidden* the past participle. This verb takes *to* or, less formally, *from*. Preferred form: "The court *forbade* the witness *to* mention insurance."

forego; forgo. The first, as suggested by the prefix, means "to go before" <the foregoing analysis>. (See **foregoing.**) The second means "to do without, pass up voluntarily, waive" <to forgo all perquisites>.

foregoing. A lawyerism to be dispensed with.

fortuitous. This word, meaning "occurring by chance," is commonly misused for *fortunate* (meaning "lucky").

forum. Pl. *forums*.

fulsome. The word means "repugnant (because overdone)," not "very full." One should not be particularly grateful for *fulsome praise*.

gauntlet; gantlet. One throws down the *gauntlet* but runs the *gantlet*.

grievous. So spelled—not *grievious*.

guilt; culpability. Strictly speaking, *guilt* is what is determined by the trier of fact; *culpability* is a matter of fact regardless of whether it ever becomes known. Learned Hand is said to have remarked that anyone can be a killer, but only a jury can make a murderer.

hale; hail. Your client was *haled* (= pulled, compelled to go) into court before the acquittal you secured was *hailed* as one of the great victories in legal history.

hanged; hung. Coats and pictures are *hung*, and sometimes even juries. But in the old days, criminals found guilty of capital offenses were *hanged*—not *hung*.

harass. So spelled.

herein; hereinafter; hereinbefore; herewith; thereof; therein; thereout; whereof; wherefore; wherein. "[It] all . . . fully appears from the affidavit of the publisher thereof heretofore herein filed."[4] You should know better. See 7.7.

hereinafter called. A stilted legalism easily avoided. Ordinarily, a shortened name unambiguously follows the full name. See 4.5.

---

4. Quoted in Penn v. Pensacola-Escambia Governmental Ctr. Auth., 311 So. 2d 97, 102 (Fla. 1975).

Poor

> Acme Fire & Casualty Company (hereinafter called "Acme")
> moves that the court dismiss the action.

Better

> Acme Fire & Casualty Company moves that the court dismiss
> the action. Acme submits that . . . .

historic; historical. The second, meaning "of, relating to, or occurring in history," is called on far more frequently <historical studies>. The first means "historically significant."

> The signing of the Declaration of Independence was a historic event.

Hobson's choice. The phrase refers not to two or more undesirable choices, but to the option of taking the one thing offered or nothing at all. Thomas Hobson, who rented horses in Cambridge, is reputed to have compelled customers to take the horse closest to the stable door or else go without. In referring to *the Hobson's choice between continuing trial with a tainted jury and facing the expense and delay of a new trial*, the writer betrays an ignorance of the source of the allusion.

hopefully. Strike this word from your vocabulary. Say *I hope* or *it is to be hoped* instead.

Poor

> Hopefully, the court will grant our writ of error.

Better

> I hope that the court will grant our writ of error.

> With luck, the court will grant our writ of error.

Cf. **thankfully.**

hung. See **hanged.**

identify. Always give this verb a direct object.

> She identified the relevant documents.

Identify with is a voguish phrase to be avoided.

Poor
> He could identify with her arguments.

Better
> He [agreed with?] [understood?] her arguments.

ideology. Often misspelled *idealogy.*

idiosyncrasy. So spelled—not *-cracy.*

i.e. See **e.g.**

if and when. Use whichever one you mean, but not both.

illegible; unreadable. *Illegible* = not plain or clear enough to be read (used of handwriting or defaced printing). *Unreadable* = too dull or obscure to be read and understood (used of bad writing).

immigrate. See **emigrate.**

imminent; eminent. The first means "impending" <imminent bodily harm>; the second, "distinguished" <Judge Friendly, the eminent jurist>.

impact (on). Avoid using *impact* as a verb. It should not displace the more traditional and less hyperbolic verbs, such as *affect* and *influence.*

Poor
> That particular precedent strongly *impacted on* the court's decision.

Better
> That particular precedent strongly *affected* the court's decision.

impinge; infringe. *Impinge* is followed by *on* or *upon*; it does not take a direct object. *Infringe*, by contrast, may either take a direct object or not:

> to infringe someone's right

to infringe on someone's rights

Though *impinge* and *infringe* are often used as if they were inter-changeable, keep in mind these connotations from the literal senses: *impinge* = to strike or dash upon something else, whereas *infringe* = to break in and thereby damage, violate, or weaken.

implement. A vogue word beloved by jargonmongers, in whose language policies and plans are *implemented.* *Carry out* is usually less vague.

imply; infer. To *imply* is to suggest; to *infer* is to deduce. The common error is to use *infer* when *imply* is the intended word.

Poor
> The circuit court's remanding the case *inferred,* in the district court's view, that plaintiff's motion for new trial should be favorably considered.

Better
> The circuit court's remanding the case *implied,* in the district court's view, that plaintiff's motion for new trial should be favorably considered.

in between. Omit *in* when the phrase is followed by an object or objects.

incident to; incidental to. The first means "closely related to; naturally appearing with"; the second means "happening by chance and subordinate to some other thing; peripheral." A properly executed codicil is *incident* to a will; an unsigned note attached to a will is treated as completely *incidental* to it.

incredulous; incredible. The first means "unbelieving; skeptical" <the verdict was so large that, when it was announced, everyone in the courtroom was incredulous>. The second means "unbelievable; not credible" <the verdict was incredibly large>.

indicate. Don't use this word where *say* or *state* or *show* will suffice.

individual. Blot out the word if *person* can serve. *Individual* contrasts a single person with a group.

Poor

> He is an odd individual.

Better

> We must protect the individual against a majoritarian tyranny.

In law, *individual* is often used to differentiate a human being from other forms of legal persons. And using the word as an adjective is safer style:

> The company had both individual and corporate shareholders.

inequity; iniquity. The first is "unfairness"; the second, "evil."

infer. See **imply.**

informant; informer. Both are used frequently, and often interchangeably. But some distinctions have begun to emerge. We usually speak (in the law of evidence) of an *informer's privilege*, but one whose information is the basis for a search warrant is called an *informant.* To the extent that a substantive distinction is possible, *informer* more often carries connotations of espionage or underhandedness, whereas *informant* may be merely a participant in a survey.

infringe. See **impinge.**

ingenious; ingenuous. These words are virtual antonyms. *Ingenious* = crafty, skillful, inventive. *Ingenuous* = artless, innocent, simple.

iniquity. See **inequity.**

in order to. Write *to,* unless the longer phrase is necessary to prevent ambiguity.

in personam. So spelled; it does not end in -*um.*

inside (of). Omit the preposition.

insure. See **assure.**

inter alia. Use *among others* where you can instead of this Latinism. Remember that *inter alia* refers to things, not people (for whom *inter alios* is the proper Latin phrase). Cf. **etc.**

interface. A jargonmonger's word; leave it to computer experts.

in terms of. In terms of writing, avoid this flotsam phrase.

Poor
> In terms of economics, the transaction failed to minimize costs.

Better
> The transaction failed to minimize costs.

irregardless. This semiliterate blend of *irrespective* and *regardless* should have been stamped out long ago. On the second day of the Supreme Court's 1986–1987 term, Chief Justice William H. Rehnquist upbraided a lawyer who used the word, saying: "I feel bound to inform you there is no word *irregardless* in the English language. The word is *regardless*."

its; it's. The possessive form of *it* is *its*; the contraction for *it is* is *it's*.

-ize. Adding this suffix to an adjective or noun is one of the most frequent means of forming new words. True, we have a number of established words such as *analogize, fertilize, harmonize, hospitalize, minimize, proselytize,* and *summarize.* But creating neologisms with *-ize* is generally to be discouraged; they are always ungainly and often superfluous. Thus, we have no real use for *accessorize, artificialize, cubiclize, fenderize* (= to fix a dented fender), *funeralize, ghettoize, Mirandize, nakedize,* and so on. The law has several legitimate curiosities ending in *-ize* (e.g., *privatize, collateralize, communitize,* and *constitutionalize*) and probably needs no more. Careful writers are wary of new words formed with this suffix. See **finalize.**

judgment. So spelled in American English and in British legal writing—not *judgement*, as in most British writing. Cf. **acknowledgment.**

judicial; judicious. *Judicious* means "well-considered, discreet, wisely circumspect" <a judicious choice>. *Judicial* may mean (1) "of, relating to, belonging to, or by the court" <judicial officers>; (2) "in court" <judicial admissions>; (3) "secularly legal" <laws of three kinds: ceremonial, judicial, and moral>; (4) "of, relating to, or fixed by a court's judgment" <an award of judicial interest>.

juncture. The phrase *at this juncture* should refer to a crisis or a critically important time; it is not equivalent merely to *at this time* or *now*. When used for either of those phrases, it is a pomposity.

juridical; jural. *Juridical* is a rather fancy and old-fashioned term meaning "relating to judicial proceedings or to the law" <"uses . . . made by judges or juridical writers of the terms"—Lord Bowen>. *Jural* may act as a synonym for *legal*, but it usually means "of or pertaining to rights and obligations" <jural relations>.

jurisprude(nt). A back-formation from *jurisprudence*, *jurisprude* originated as a jocular word referring to a lawyer who regards the law with excessive (prudish) veneration. Today, however, the word is often used in a neutral sense. But *jurisprudent*, a noun meaning "a jurist, or learned lawyer," is the better word when you don't intend pejorative connotations.

jurist = a learned lawyer. The word is not a synonym for *judge*, though many judges are jurists.

just deserts. So spelled, but trite.

kind of; sort of. These are just informal, wordy substitutes for *somewhat, rather, somehow*, and other weaselly adverbs. If you need one of these hedging adverbs, use a one-word form—that is, instead of *kind of short*, write *rather short*. But *kind* and *sort* may properly function as nouns in phrases such as *this kind of lawsuit*. See **these kind.**

kudos. Derived from the Greek *kydos* ("glory"), *kudos* is a singular noun meaning "praise, glory."

The kudos she received was nonpartisan.

The word is often mistakenly thought to be plural. *Kudo,* a false singular, has come to plague many texts.

lay. See **lie.**

lease; let. *Let,* dating from the 10th century, is actually 300 years older than *lease* in the sense "to grant the temporary possession and use of (land, buildings, rooms, etc.) to another in consideration of rent." So both are well established. But *lease* is more common today.

legible. See **illegible.**

less; fewer. *Less* applies to mass nouns such as *salt, stress,* and *trouble. Fewer* applies to count nouns such as *calories, books,* and *people. Less* for *fewer* is an all-too-frequent error.

Poor
> This rule also provides that if three or *less* jurors become disabled or otherwise unable to serve, the remaining jurors may render a verdict.

Better
> This rule also provides that if three or *fewer* jurors become disabled or otherwise unable to serve, the remaining jurors may render a verdict.

let. See **lease.**

liable; likely; apt. Don't use *liable* (= subject to or exposed to) merely for *likely* (= expected, probably) or *apt* (= inclined toward, fit). *Liable* best refers to an unpleasant occurrence that risks being permanent or recurrent.

Poor
> The plaintiff is liable to prevail in this lawsuit.

Better

> The plaintiff is likely to prevail in this lawsuit.
>
> The stock market is liable to fluctuations.
>
> Humpty Dumpty is liable to fall.

Liable may also mean "responsible, subject to liability," and is usually confined to civil contexts in American English, though in British English the word appears in criminal as well as civil contexts <criminally liable>.

libel. See **defamation**.

lie; lay. Very simply, *lie* (= to recline, be situated) is intransitive and therefore doesn't take a direct object <he lies on his bed>, whereas *lay* (= to put down, arrange) is transitive and therefore demands a direct object <he laid his hand on her shoulder> <they laid the body in its grave>. The verbs are inflected *lie* > *lay* > *lain* and *lay* > *laid* > *laid*.

like. In standard usage, *like* is a preposition that governs nouns and noun phrases, not a conjunction that governs verbs or clauses.

Poor

> He argued this case like he argued the previous one.

Better

> He argued this case as he argued the previous one.

If we change *argue* to *argument*, thereby making a noun phrase out of what had been a clause, *like* is appropriate:

> His argument in this case was *like* his argument in the previous one.

likely. See **liable**.

literally. *Literally* (= with truth to the letter, exactly) is not a good word for introducing metaphors. The word can literally make a liar of you.

Poor
> The judge had sat literally glued to the bench.

Better
> The judge had sat glued to the bench.

loan; lend. In formal usage, it's best to use *lend* as the verb and *loan* as the noun. *Loan* is considered permissible, however, when used as a verb denoting the lending of money (as distinguished from the lending of other things).

The verbs are inflected *loan > loaned > loaned* and *lend > lent > lent*.

loath; loathe. *Loath*, an adjective, means "reluctant"; *loathe*, a verb, means "to abhor, detest."

mad. A casualism when used for *angry*.

make reference to. Verbose for *refer to*. See 7.11.

manner, in a _____. This is the long way of expressing an adverb. When possible, use an adverb ending in -*ly*, such as *tortiously* rather than *in a tortious manner*.

masterful; masterly. The master in *masterful* is opposed to *servant* or *slave*; the master in *masterly* is opposed to *unskilled worker*. A boorish tyrant is *masterful*; a great artist is *masterly*.

material; relevant. These terms are distinguished in the law of evidence. *Material* = having some logical connection with the consequential facts. *Relevant* = tending to prove or disprove a matter in issue.

may. See **can.**

meaningful. This word, meaning "full of meaning or expression," is becoming a meaningless buzzword, especially when used for *reasonable*.

Poor

> The options will expire a *meaningful* time before the conversion date.

Better

> The options will expire a *reasonable* time before the conversion date.

The word has also been used to mean "significant, important," as here:

Poor

> We find no *meaningful* constitutional infraction.

Better

> We find no *significant* constitutional infraction.

These uses have rendered *meaningful* a vogue word that careful writers avoid. See 2.15.

medium. The usual plural is *media,* which preferably takes a plural verb <the media were accurate in their reporting>. *Mediums* is the correct plural when the sense is "clairvoyants, spiritualists."

militate. See **mitigate.**

minuscule. So spelled—not *miniscule.*

mischievous. So spelled—not *mischievious.*

mitigate; militate. *Mitigate* = to make less severe or intense. *Militate* = to exert a strong influence. *Mitigate against* is incorrect for *militate against,* as here:

Poor

> This consideration *mitigates against* immediate review.

Better

> This consideration *militates against* immediate review.

Edmund Wilson called this "William Faulkner's favorite error";[5] here, as in other ways, Faulkner is no model for the legal writer.

momentarily. The word means "for a moment," not "in a moment."

moneys, moneyed. So spelled. Avoid *monies* and *monied.*

moot. This adjective once meant only "debatable" (a moot point was one legitimately the subject of argument), but now it most commonly means "having no practical significance" (a moot issue being one that a court need not decide).

As for the verb, to *moot* a point is either (1) to offer it for discussion, or (2) to take away its practical significance.

more important(ly). As an introductory phrase, *more important* has long been considered an elliptical form of "What is more important . . ."; hence, the -*ly* form is thought to be the less desirable one.

Poor
> This provision directly conflicts with section 1235(k); *more importantly,* section 1273(a) defeats Montana's right to the funds collected on the ceded strip as much as it defeats that of the tribe.

Better
> This provision directly conflicts with section 1235(k); *more important,* section 1273(a) defeats Montana's right to the funds collected on the ceded strip as much as it defeats that of the tribe.

mortgagor. So spelled, even though the final -*g*- is a soft one (sounded as a -*j*-).

multiplicitous. So spelled—not *multiplicious.*

mutual. See **common.**

myself. Use the word reflexively:

---

5. Edmund Wilson, The Bit Between My Teeth 570 (1965).

I therefore recuse myself.

I need not fear incriminating myself.

Or use it as an intensive:

I myself will sue the corporation on behalf of the class of persons harmed.

But don't make *myself* substitute for *I* or *me*, as in *My partner and myself would like to meet with you.* (That should be *My partner and I....*) Using *myself* in that way is no less direct than *I* or *me.* And it sounds doltish. See 2.22.

nature, of a _____. Always wordy.

Poor
    This was a case of an unusual nature.

Better
    This was an unusual case.

necessary; necessitous. *Necessary,* the more common word, means "essential." *Necessitous* = placed or living in a condition of necessity or poverty; hard up.

neither. See **nor** and 3.5 (pp. 71–73).

noisome. This is sometimes misconstrued as meaning "noisy, clamorous." The word means "noxious, malodorous," and is related etymologically to *annoy.*

If the house is to be cleaned, it is for those who occupy and govern it, rather than for strangers, to do the *noisome* work. (Cardozo)

none. This term means (1) "not one," or (2) "not any." So it may correctly take either a singular or plural verb <none was present> <none were present>, depending on the writer's intention. *None was* is the more emphatic form.

nor; or. *Neither* should be followed by *nor,* and *either* should be followed by *or.*

neither this nor that

She can neither stand nor walk.

either Brandeis or Holmes

When the alternatives are singular, the verb should be in the singular.

Neither the Federalist Society nor the National Organization for Women supports the nomination.

But when one of the alternatives is singular and the other plural, the last noun or noun phrase determines the number of the verb.

Neither I nor they *were* present at the meeting.

Either they or she *was* required to submit a report.

You're typically better off putting the plural form last. So that last example might be improved: *Either she or they were required to submit a report.*

null and void. A venial redundancy for *null* or *void.*

numerous. Stuffy for *many.*

observance; observation. *Observance* = heeding, obeying; the act of following a custom or rule <observance of the term of the contract>. *Observation* = scrutiny, study; a judgment or inference from what one has seen. One whose observance of the distinction is slipshod will be thought to lack observation in reading good prose.

obviously; certainly; clearly; undeniably. It has become an ironic joke among lawyers that when an opponent—or for that matter, frequently, a judge—uses one of these words, the statement that follows is likely to be false, unreasonable, or fraught with doubt. This skepticism has grown from the widespread abuse of the terms. Reserve them for what is truly obvious, certain, clear, or undeniable. When they are used merely to buttress arguments, they take on the character of weasel words: they weaken the arguments. See 2.18, 7.12.

occurrence. So spelled.

off of. Omit *of.*

of which. See **whose.**

one another. See **each other.**

one . . . his. This wording is inferior to *one . . . one's.* The infelicity is not uncommon.

> *Poor*
>> A constructive trust arises when one obtains the legal title to property in violation of his duty to another.

> *Better*
>> A constructive trust arises when one obtains the legal title to property in violation of one's duty to another.

one of those (+ plural noun) who (or *that*). This wording takes a plural verb, not a singular one.

> *Poor*
>> This is one of the admiralty texts that is worth reading.

> *Better*
>> This is one of the admiralty texts that are worth reading.

The reason for the plural verb becomes apparent when we reword the sentence:

> Of the admiralty texts that are worth reading, this is one.

oneself. So spelled—no longer *one's self.*

only. Though we have old exceptions (heaven only knows how many), in written English the best placement of *only* is directly before the words to be limited by it. The more words separating *only* from its correct position, the more awkward the sentence and the greater the probability of ambiguity.

Poor
> A pro se complaint can *only* be dismissed for failure to state a claim if it appears beyond doubt that the plaintiff can prove no set of facts in support of the claim.

Better
> A pro se complaint can be dismissed for failure to state a claim *only* if it appears beyond doubt that the plaintiff can prove no set of facts in support of the claim.

on the part of. Write *by.*

or. See **nor** and 3.5 (pp. 71–73).

oral. See **verbal.**

orientate. Use the verb *orient,* not its overgrown sibling.

otherwise. This word creates more run-on sentences in English than any other. It may begin a sentence or follow a semicolon, but it should virtually never follow a comma.

Poor
> Liability fastens on the principal when the agent is *negligent, otherwise* there is no liability.

Better
> Liability fastens on the principal when the agent is *negligent; otherwise,* there is no liability.

outside of. Omit *of.*

overly. Strike this word from your vocabulary. Though it is old, *overly* is almost always unnecessary because *over-* may be prefixed at will: *overbroad, overrefined, overoptimistic, overreached,* and so on. If *over-* seems awkward in any given combination, resort to *too* or *unduly* (*too harsh,* for example, instead of *overharsh*).

panacea. A cure-all, not just any remedy.

parameters. Technical contexts aside, this jargonistic vogue word is not used by those with a heightened sensitivity to language. When you can discern what this mush-word means in a given context, you see immediately that it has displaced a far simpler and more straightforward term (*limits, criteria, considerations*).

Poor
> The terms of the state's consent to be sued define the *parameters* of the court's jurisdiction to entertain suit.

Better
> The terms of the state's consent to be sued define the *limits* of the court's jurisdiction to entertain suit.

partially; partly. Whenever either word might suffice, choose *partly* (= in part, to some extent). We say, for example, that someone is *partly to blame* or that the architecture of a building is *partly influenced* by the work of Frank Lloyd Wright. *Partially* is the better form only when you refer to a condition or state <partially dependent> <partially impaired vision>.

pejorative. So spelled—not *perjorative*.

percent. One word.

perpetuate; perpetrate. The first means "to prolong or make last (often in perpetuity)" <to perpetuate traditions>; the second means "to commit or carry out" <to perpetrate a fraud>. *Perpetuate* is connotatively neutral <perpetuating folkways, perpetuating the fallacy>, whereas *perpetrate* is usually pejorative <perpetrating fraud and other crimes>.

personally. This word often appears unnecessarily.

Poor
> I personally think that the statute bars governmental liability.

Better
   I think that the statute bars governmental liability.

phase; faze. The first is a vague word that you should have already struck from your working vocabulary (see 2.14). The second is a verb meaning "to disturb or disconcert."

   But the defeat hardly fazed those who were unshakable in their moral certitude.

plan on [go]ing. Write, for example, *plan to go.*

plead. The better past-tense and past-participial form is *pleaded,* not *pled.*

practical; practicable. *Practical* = manifested in practice; capable of being put to good use <a practical guide to the law of charter-parties>. *Practicable* = capable of being accomplished, feasible, possible <a practicable method of desegregation>.

practice; practise. In American English, the first is both the noun and verb. In British English, the first is the noun; the second, the verb.

precipitous; precipitate. These words are different, though often confused. *Precipitous* = like a precipice; steep <a precipitous decline in enrollment>. *Precipitate* = sudden, hasty, rash, showing violent or uncontrollable speed <an unfortunately precipitate ruling>. (As a verb, *precipitate* is a fancy way of saying "to cause" or "to bring about.")

predominately. This term is inferior to *predominantly.*

prefer . . . than. This is wrong. *Prefer* takes *to* or *over.*

   We prefer legal arguments to emotional jeremiads.

   She said she preferred litigating over practicing corporate law.

preliminary to. Write *before.*

preparatory to. A legalism for *in preparation for* or *to prepare for.*

prescribe; proscribe. These near-antonyms are sometimes confused. To *prescribe* is to lay down (a rule), to dictate. To *proscribe* is to prohibit.

presently. This one-word ambiguity may mean "immediately," "after a short time," or "at present, currently." If the word is not clear to a would-be misreader of your prose, don't use it.

presumptive; presumptuous. The first means (1) "giving reasonable grounds for presumption or belief" or (2) "based on a presumption or inference." The second means "arrogant, presuming."

previous to. Write *before.*

principal; principle. In nonlegal usage, *principal* (= chief, primary) is ordinarily an adjective, and *principle* (= a truth, law, doctrine, or course of action) is almost always a noun. The exceptions for *principal* have to do with short-form phrases: *principal* for *principal person,* as in a school or in the law of agency; and *principal* for *principal investment* in the context of banking and trusts.

prioritize. Unmitigated jargon. Don't *prioritize; set* or *make priorities.*

prior to. Write *before.*

proof; evidence; testimony. *Proof* is evidence found to be conclusive. *Evidence* is any means by which an alleged fact in issue might be established or disproved; thus, *evidence* may include documents and tangible objects in addition to *testimony,* which refers only to oral evidence given by a witness.

prophecy; prophesy. The first is the noun <a prophecy of a good fortune>; the second, the verb <he prophesied good fortune for the appellant>.

proscribe. See **prescribe.**

protagonist. Literally, the word means "the chief character in a drama"; derivatively, it means "a champion of a cause." Don't use *protagonist* to refer to just any supporter of a cause or to a champion of something less than a cause.

Poor

> The complexity of the community-property system is not offset by those values claimed for the system by its most ardent *protagonists.*

Better

> The complexity of the community-property system is not offset by those values claimed for the system by its most ardent *proponents.*

Legal writers sometimes err by calling both sides to a lawsuit the *protagonists,* probably because it sounds much softer than *antagonists.*

Poor

> This proceeding is the culmination of a struggle between state and federal sovereigns. The *protagonists* are the Massachusetts Department of Education and the United States Department of Education.

Better

> This proceeding is the culmination of a struggle between state and federal sovereigns. The *antagonists* [or *parties*] are the Massachusetts Department of Education and the United States Department of Education.

protectible. So spelled.

proved; proven. As a past participle, *proved* is the better form <he had proved all the elements of the prima facie case>. *Proven* is the participial adjective <the proven elements of the claim>. It is, however, established as a past participle in the not-guilty verdict in Scots law, "not proven."

provided that. This phrase should be unceremoniously buried. See 2.28.

publicly. So spelled—not *publically*.

purposely; purposefully; purposively. What is done *purposely* is done on purpose.

> He purposely set the building on fire.

What is done *purposefully* is done for a particular purpose.

> The court purposefully avoided the constitutional question.

What is done *purposively* is done to serve a useful function, though not as a result of planning.

> Over the years, the city purposively controlled the flow of north–south traffic.

pursuant to. Write *under, in accordance with, as required by, in response to,* or *in carrying out.* These are ordinary English words and phrases; *pursuant to* is pure legalese.

question as to whether; question of whether. Write *question whether.*

quote. This has traditionally been a verb. As a noun, it's a casualism. In formal writing, *quotation* is the better noun.

raise; rise. *Raise,* as a transitive verb, takes an object:

> They raised no objections.

Rise, as an intransitive verb, takes no object:

> The sun also rises.

The verbs are inflected *raise > raised > raised* and *rise > rose > risen.*

readable. See **illegible**.

reason . . . is because. This wording is verbose and incorrect; *because* and *reason* each imply the sense of the other. The best solution is usually to strike out *reason* and *is.*

Poor

> The *reason* such matters are not material and need not be disclosed *is because* public disclosure of tentative, indefinite, and contingent facts would itself be misleading.

Better

> Such matters are not material and need not be disclosed *because* public disclosure of tentative, indefinite, and contingent facts would itself be misleading.

If you must stay with the *reason . . . is* formula, follow with *that* rather than *because*.

recur; reoccur. The first means "to happen again and again, often at predictable intervals." The second means merely "to happen again."

refer back. A venial redundancy; *refer* alone is almost always sufficient.

refute. This is not synonymous with *deny, rebut,* or *contradict.* It means "to disprove or overcome conclusively."

regard as (being). *Being* is unnecessary here.

regrettable; regretful. We regret what is *regrettable*; and in so doing we are *regretful.* Here the words are used correctly:

> She regretfully admitted deceiving Congress in her testimony, calling the deception merely "regrettable."

relevant. See **material.**

remand back. Drop the second word.

reoccur. See **recur.**

repeat again. Unless you mean "to repeat a second time" (i.e., do it a third time), this is a redundancy.

reputation. See **character.**

rescission. So spelled.

res gestae. Literally, "things done"; this term denotes either the events with which a court is concerned or other contemporaneous events. No reputable writer on evidence has kind words for this phrase because it is incorrigibly vague: "The ancient phrase can well be jettisoned."[6]

respect. Replace the phrases *with respect to* and *in respect of* with simpler expressions, such as single prepositions.

Poor

> The issue with respect to liability is whether the defendant intended to harm the plaintiff.

Better

> The issue of liability depends on whether the defendant intended to harm the plaintiff.

Better Yet

> The defendant's liability depends on whether he intended to harm the plaintiff.

respective(ly). Often unnecessary.

Poor

> Each shareholder is then to be paid his or her *respective* share of the dividends.

Better

> Each shareholder is then to be paid his or her share of the dividends.

Never use the word *respective* or *respectively* without first determining whether the sentence says the same thing without it.

Poor

> Justice O'Connor and Justice Scalia respectively filed concurrences.

---

6. E.W. CLEARY, MCCORMICK ON EVIDENCE § 288, at 836 (3d ed. 1984).

Better
> Justice O'Connor and Justice Scalia [both] filed concurrences.

restive. This word is almost an antonym of *restful*, with which it is sometimes confused. *Restive* = restless, impatient, refractory.

rise. See **raise.**

sacrilegious. So spelled.

said, adj. The most baneful word in legaldegook, *said* should always be avoided when it would merely displace *the, that, this,* or any other such pointing word. Does anyone believe that the following passage has become more precise because of the pervasiveness of *said*?

> A considerable number of persons were attracted to *said* square by *said* meeting, and *said* bombs and other fireworks which were being exploded there. A portion of the center of the square about 40 to 60 feet was roped off by the police of *said* Chelsea, and *said* bombs or shells were fired off within the space so enclosed, and no spectators were allowed to be within *said* inclosure. The plaintiffs were lawfully in *said* highway at the time of the explosion of *said* mortar, and near *said* ropes, and were in the exercise of due care.

same, n. A sorry substitute for a pronoun.

Poor
> Upon examining the statute, we find same to be ambiguous.

Better
> Upon examining the statute, we find it to be ambiguous.

sanction. This verb is ambiguous because it may mean either (1) "to approve" <to sanction her conduct> or (2) "to penalize" <to sanction defendant's counsel for dilatory tactics>. Be sure that the context makes the sense clear.

sensual; sensuous. *Sensual* has to do with lust and physical pleasures <sensual pursuits>; *sensuous*, with the five senses <sensuous perceptions>.

shall; will. Grammarians formerly relied on the following paradigm:
Simple Futurity

	Singular	*Plural*
First Person	I shall	we shall
Second Person	you will	you will
Third Person	he will	they will

Determination, Promise, or Command

	Singular	*Plural*
First Person	I will	we will
Second Person	you shall	you shall
Third Person	he shall	they shall

You might have struggled to learn this years ago (and it would have been a struggle!). But since it doesn't reflect the way the language is used—or ever has been used—you'd be better off forgetting it. If you're using American English, you won't need *shall* much—except in posing playful questions such as, "Shall we dance?" Stick to *will*.

But what about legal drafting, a field in which *shall* traditionally denotes commands? The answer is that this is a half-truth. Literally. At least half the *shalls* in modern drafting don't command at all: they're future-tense *shalls*, permissive *shalls*, or other types of *shalls*. If you want to retain *shall*, then make sure that in each sentence in which it appears, it's the equivalent of *must*. Otherwise, cut it. Once you've started revising by this principle, you'll probably decide that it's easier simply to cut all your *shalls*. Those that are mandatory you can consistently replace with *must* or (in contracts) *will* or *agrees to*.[7]

slander. See **defamation.**

---

7. *See* BRYAN A. GARNER, A DICTIONARY OF MODERN LEGAL USAGE 939–42 (2d ed. 1995).

stationary; stationery. The first is an adjective meaning "at rest." The second is a noun referring to writing paper. A *stationer* supplies such paper, and remembering that the agent noun ends in -*er* may help you keep the two words straight.

struck; stricken. The preferred past participle is *struck.*

The objectionable remarks were struck from the record.

Stricken should be confined to the sense "afflicted with" <a community stricken with AIDS>. *Stricken* is also used as an adjective:

her stricken remarks

their stricken faces

subsequent to. Use *after.*

such. Properly used to mean "of this kind" <such an appeal>, *such* is deplorable as a substitute for *this* or *these* or *the* <such appeal>. Sir Frederick Pollock tried unsuccessfully to "choke off" this bit of legalese during the last century;[8] may we finally succeed where he failed.

sui generis; sui juris. The first means "unique, one of a kind"; the second means "of full age and capacity." See 7.8.

supersede. The last syllable of this word, whose correct spelling is one of the indicia of the careful writer, is -*sede*, not -*cede.*

testimony. See **proof.**

thankfully. The same demon that has made *hopefully* mean "I hope" has now attacked *thankfully.* The word means "gratefully, in a manner expressing thanks," but by slipshod extension has come to be used as here:

---

8. *See* 2 HOLMES–POLLOCK LETTERS 251 (Mark DeWolfe Howe ed., 1941).

Thankfully, it didn't rain yesterday.

Avoid this usage. Cf. **hopefully.**

that; which. The distinction eludes otherwise brilliant minds. Restrictive relative clauses, which most properly begin with *that,* are not set off by commas. This kind of clause is essential to grammatical and logical completeness:

> The fact that most swayed Judge Wilson was the defendants' destruction of evidence.

Nonrestrictive relative clauses, which most properly begin with *which,* are set off by commas. This kind of clause is so loosely connected with the essential meaning of the sentence that it might have been omitted without a change in that essential meaning:

> The Supreme Court, [which is] the forum of last resort in the federal system, is the only court established by the Constitution.

The simplest test for determining the type of relative clause is this: if putting the clause in parentheses leaves the basic meaning of the sentence intact, the clause is nonrestrictive (properly introduced by *which*). If the sentence is rendered nonsensical in context when the clause is put in parentheses, or gives the sentence an entirely different sense, then it is restrictive (properly introduced by *that*).

> The court that overturned the case is now defunct.

> The court, which overturned the case, is now defunct.

In the first sentence, the court is defined or identified by the fact that it overturned a certain case; it has not been previously discussed with any particularity. In the second sentence, the court must already be known, and the fact that it overturned the case is merely thrown in as incidental information.

To illustrate further, with dialogue:

> "Paris, which has a population of about 23,000, is the city closest to Pecan Gap."

"I thought Paris was a major international city!"

"That's a different one. The Paris that has only 23,000 people is in East Texas."

therefore; therefor. The first means "as a consequence, it must follow that"; the second means "for it, for that." *Therefor* typifies legalese. Replace it with the simpler expression.

Poor
> The order surprised both parties, and the court gave no reason therefor.

Better
> The order surprised both parties, and the court gave no reason for it.

there is; there are. If assertion of existence is important, *there is* or *there are* may prove necessary.

There was enough water in the creek to float a battleship.

But often these are weak introductory phrases.

Poor
> There are three reasons why that case should be overruled.

Better
> That case should be overruled for three reasons.

thereof; therein; thereout. See **herein**.

these kind; those kind. These are illogical expressions. Write *this kind* or *these kinds*, depending on the sense. See **kind of**.

this. The word should always have a clear, single-phrase antecedent.

Poor
> Although statutes in derogation of the common law are to be strictly construed, *this* does not mean that the statute should be given the narrowest possible meaning.

Better

> *The maxim that statutes in derogation of the common law are to be strictly construed* does not mean that they are to be given the narrowest possible meaning.

Among the many possible rewordings, the one just illustrated is underused in legal writing: making what began as a concessive phrase (*Although . . . construed*) the subject of the sentence rather than *this*, which was supposed to refer to the entire concessive phrase.

thusly. A semiliterate version of *thus*, which is itself an adverb.

till; until. These are equally acceptable in formal English. Yet many writers mistakenly consider *till* a casualism, or fall into error by writing *'til* or *'till*.

too. The word is both an intensive <too strict> and a connective <that appeal, too, was rejected>.

tortious; tortuous; torturous. The first corresponds to the legal word *tort*, the last to an illegal practice, torture. *Tortuous*, which is not derived from a shorter English noun, means "twisting, turning, winding."

> a tortuous path through the hills

> a tortuous line of legal reasoning

transpire. Literally "to breathe across," this word has traditionally meant "to become known" <as the facts transpired at trial>, not "to happen." To write about what actually transpired is to engage in loose usage.

try and. Avoid this expression in favor of the infinitive: *try to win.*

unbeknown(st). *Unbeknown* is the better form.

undeniably. See **obviously.**

unique. Reserve this word for what is one of a kind. The loose usage is to write *unique* when you mean merely *interesting* or *unusual* or *novel.*

unreadable. See **illegible.**

until. See **till.**

utilize. A turgid word for the verb *use,* just as *utilization* is for the noun *use.*

venal; venial. The first, used of a person, means "susceptible to bribery" <venal petty officers>. The second means "pardonable, excusable" <venial lapses in morality>.

verbal; oral. The first is broader than the second. What is spoken is *oral.* What is written or spoken—that is, expressed in words—is *verbal.*

very. Intended to strengthen a statement, this adjective often does just the opposite. Writers do well to eliminate nine of every ten uses.

viable. The word originally meant "capable of living; able to maintain a separate existence" <a viable fetus> and was extended to figurative uses in reference to immaterial objects or concepts.

> The doctrine cannot breathe life into a lawsuit that is not otherwise viable.

Avoid using the word as a synonym for *feasible* or *practicable.*

virtually. A weasel word.

viz. Use *namely.*

whereas. This word, used again and again in the recitals of a contract, is the archetypal legalism. Banish it from contracts: use straightforward, complete sentences instead. In its literary sense, as a near-synonym of *although,* or *but by contrast,* the word is entirely acceptable.

whereof; wherein; wherefore. See **herein.**

whether [or not]. Usually, *whether* suffices without *or not.*

which. See **that.**

while. The word may be used for *although* or *whereas*, despite what purists say about its inherent temporality. *While* is, however, the more relaxed and conversational term.

> *While* terseness is a virtue too often lacking in judicial opinions, there is no better precaution against judicial mistakes than the setting out accurately and adequately [of] the material facts as well as the points to be decided.[9]

who; whom. The distinction to keep in mind is that *who* acts as the subject of a verb <the person who is talking>, *whom* as the object of a verb or preposition <the person of whom we spoke>. Sometimes it is tricky business keeping the verb in sight:

> If the servant, without authority, entrusts the instrumentality to one *who*, on account of his age, inexperience, or recklessness, he has reason to believe *is* likely to harm others, the master would be liable.

In that sentence, *who* is correct because it acts as the subject of *is*; the intervening words should not throw us off the scent.

whose; of which. *Which*, unfortunately, has no other possessive form than *of which*:

> They established the tenancy, the continuance of which depends on . . . .

Therefore, the possessive *whose* is sometimes used of things as well as persons:

> They established the tenancy, whose continuance depends on . . . .

---

9. CHARLES EVANS HUGHES, THE SUPREME COURT OF THE UNITED STATES 64 (1928).

whosoever, whomsoever, etc. Simplify legalisms of this kind: *whoever, whomever,* etc.

willful; wilful. *Willful* is the preferred spelling in American English, *wilful* in British English. *Willfull* is a misspelling.

-wise. Make it one of your basic tenets not to use this suffix, with or without hyphens, in newfangled combinations such as *taxwise, costwise,* and *liability-wise.* Established words such as *clockwise, lengthwise,* and *likewise* are perfectly acceptable.

withal. Now a useless archaism.

within, adj. To refer to *the within memorandum* is to be guilty of legaldegook. Write *the enclosed memorandum.*

with respect to. See **respect.**

would. To say *I would submit* or *I would argue* unnecessarily removes your statement from immediacy. Under what circumstances would you submit or argue? Unless you are stating what you would argue in a hypothetical argument (something that few apart from law professors do), don't weaken your statements by using the conditional *would.* See 2.17.

SIX

Rhetorical Figures in Law

"Why," Jack Balkin asks, "do we believe that logical argument is hermetically sealed off from the vagaries of language—from the subtle but insidious influence of surface characteristics of language, such as metaphor, rhyming, etymological and phonic similarity? . . . Why could a system of legal argument not rely on literary features of language, on puns and plays on words?"[1]

It can. Our own system of legal argument already does so and has long been at it. Many of our most gifted legal writers have used figures of speech, or "graces of language"—not just insidious vagaries—to give their prose greater force. Figures of speech help make writing something more than serviceable; they help make it memorable.

Perhaps Lord Macmillan "put the case a little too high" when he said that "no advocate can be a great pleader who has not a sense of literary form and whose mind is not stored with the treasures of our great literary inheritance upon which he may draw at will."[2] But the kernel of the truth remains: familiarity with literary forms of English will strengthen your handling of language.

---

1. J.M. Balkin, *The Footnote*, 83 Nw. U. L. Rev. 275, 317 (1989).
2. Lord Macmillan (as quoted in Norman Birkett, Six Great Advocates 108 (1961)).

The following pages show some of the common rhetorical figures used by legal stylists. Several examples illustrate more than one figure. Since literary devices are the most readily learned discursive skills, they merit close study. We're bound to imitate in some measure, and we should therefore take care that we imitate good models—our great predecessors and contemporaries—not the proliferating bad ones. Studying the passages quoted in this chapter may help you learn and remember the many structures and devices available as you compose.

Figures of speech are to be used only when they achieve the particular effect—a special emphasis or an aphoristic quality—that you require. Many of them are appropriate primarily in elevated writing, as the quoted passages suggest. If you were to pack your prose with them, without regard to what you were saying and why, you would achieve only an unintended humor. Experiment cautiously: the plainest possible style is far superior to one that is artificially decorated with figures of speech.

Don't bother to memorize all the Greek names; they serve merely as conventional labels for the various species.

COMPARISON

6.1 Metaphor: "transferring." An implicit comparison between two things of unlike nature that nevertheless have something in common. A metaphor says not that a thing is like something else, but that it is that something else. "The novice usually ignores the metaphor; the experienced writer cherishes it,"[3] because it is pictorial and often witty.

> The law has "its epochs of ebb and flow." One of the flood seasons is upon us. Men are insisting, as perhaps never before, that law shall be made true to its ideal of justice. Let us gather up the driftwood, and leave the waters pure.
>
> Benjamin N. Cardozo, *A Ministry of Justice*,
> 35 Harv. L. Rev. 113, 126 (1921)

---

3. Percy Marks, The Craft of Writing 120 (1932).

Juries are not leaves swayed by every breath.

> L. Hand, J., in *United States v. Garsson*,
> 291 F. 646, 649 (S.D.N.Y. 1923)

A judge should ask himself the question how, if the makers of the Act had themselves come across this ruck in the texture of it, would they have straightened it out? He must then do as they would have done. A judge must not alter the material of which the Act is woven, but he can and should iron out the creases.

> Denning, L.J., in *Seaford Court Estates Ltd v. Asher*
> [1949] 2 K.B. 481, 499

[T]he average law review writer, scorning the common bludgeon and reaching into his style for a rapier, finds himself trying to wield a barn door.

> Fred Rodell, *Goodbye to Law Reviews—Revisited*,
> 48 Va. L. Rev. 279, 281 (1962)

Modern jurisprudence trenches on the fields of the social sciences and of philosophy; it digs into the historical past and attempts to create the symmetry of a garden out of the luxuriant chaos of conflicting legal systems.

> G.W. Paton, *A Textbook of Jurisprudence* 1
> (G.W. Paton & D.P. Derham eds., 4th ed. 1972)

Try to hear all the reverberations that a metaphor will set off in the minds of readers. If your metaphor does something preposterous such as driving judges to suicide—as in the example that follows—you'd better start over:

> [T]he statement of the case is a place where one leads the judge right to the edge of the cliff which represents the theme and then allows the judge to jump off herself rather than the attorney trying to shove her over.
>
> Randy Lee, *Writing the Statement of the Case*,
> 10 Whittier L. Rev. 619, 626 (1989)

6.2 Personification: "face-making." The human embodiment of an abstraction; making (something nonhuman) into a person.

Personification is a special type of metaphor. We frequently personify the law, as Ronald Dworkin has observed: "Lawyers . . . talk about what the law 'says' or whether the law is 'silent' about some issue or other."[4] Here are two quite different personifications of law broadly conceived, followed by a narrower example personifying a particular holding.

> The law is a fat man walking down the street in a high hat. And far be it from the law reviews to be any party to the chucking of a snowball or a judicious placing of a banana-peel.
>
> Fred Rodell, *Goodbye to Law Reviews—Revisited*,
> 48 Va. L. Rev. 279, 281 (1962)

> When I think thus of the Law, I see a princess mightier than she who once wrought at Bayeux, eternally weaving into her web dim figures of the ever-lengthening past—figures too dim to be noticed by the idle, too symbolic to be interpreted except by her pupils, but to the discerning eye disclosing every painful step and every world-shaking contest by which mankind has worked and fought its way from savage isolation to organic social life.
>
> But we who are here know the Law even better in another aspect. We see her daily, not as anthropologists, not as students and philosophers, but as actors in a drama of which she is the providence and overruling power. When I think of the Law as we know her in the courthouse and the market, she seems to me a woman sitting by the wayside, beneath whose overshadowing hood every man shall see the countenance of his deserts or needs. The timid and overborne gain heart from her protecting smile. Fair combatants, manfully standing to their rights, see her keeping the lists with the stern and discriminating eye of even justice. The wretch who has defied her most sacred commands, and has thought to creep through ways where she was not, finds his path ends with her, and beholds beneath her hood the inexorable face of death.
>
> . . . [W]hen for the first time I was called to speak on such an occasion as this, the only thought that could come into my mind, the

---

4. RONALD DWORKIN, LAW'S EMPIRE 4 (1986).

only feeling that could fill my heart, the only words that could spring to my lips, were a hymn to her in whose name we are met here tonight—to our mistress, the Law.

>   Oliver Wendell Holmes, "The Law,"
>   in *Collected Legal Papers* 25, 27–28 (1920; repr. 1952)

The rule in *Andrews v. Partington* is a somewhat battered veteran, but it still remains on its feet after upwards of 200 years.

>   Jenkins, L.J., in *In re Bleckly* [1951] Ch. 740, 751

6.3 Simile [sim-i-lee]: "likening one thing to another." A comparison made usually by means of *like* or *as*; hence, an explicit comparison, as opposed to the implicit comparison of a metaphor. Remember the advice of E.B. White: "The simile is a common device and a useful one, but similes coming in rapid fire, one right on top of another, are more distracting than illuminating. Readers need time to catch their breath; they can't be expected to compare everything with something else, and no relief in sight."[5]

To say that all men are sometimes dishonest means only that no one can live outside of himself and those around him. He may choose what seems to him the honest way, but his nature and his life can stand only a certain pressure—when that is reached he resists no more. He may be likened to a steam boiler. Some boilers are safe at twenty pounds pressure to the square inch, but will break at forty. The boiler is neither honest nor dishonest—it stands a certain pressure, and no more. Man cannot be classified as honest or dishonest—he goes along with the game of life and can stand a certain pressure for the sake of his ideals, but at a certain point he can stand no more.

>   Clarence Darrow, "Is Man Fundamentally Dishonest?,"
>   in *Verdicts Out of Court* 295, 301 (1963)

[P]rocedure courses [in law school] appear as the technical tools of the trade and nothing more; as books of etiquette through which

---

5. WILLIAM STRUNK JR. & E.B. WHITE, THE ELEMENTS OF STYLE 80 (4th ed. 1980).

one learns to use the legal oyster fork for legal oysters and to avoid the knife when picking bones from legal fish.

Karl Llewellyn, *The Bramble Bush* 17 (1930; repr. 1951)

Legal learning is largely built around the principle known as stare decisis. It means that on the same point of law yesterday's decision shall govern today's decision. Like a coral reef, the common law thus becomes a structure of fossils.

Robert H. Jackson, *The Struggle for Judicial Supremacy*
295 (1941)

The position of a judge has been likened to that of an oyster—anchored in one place, unable to take the initiative, unable to go out after things, restricted to working on and digesting what the fortuitous eddies and currents of litigation may wash his way.

Calvert Magruder, *Mr. Justice Brandeis,* 55 Harv. L. Rev. 193, 194
(1941)

To see him preside was like witnessing Toscanini lead an orchestra.

Felix Frankfurter, *Chief Justices I Have Known,*
39 Va. L. Rev. 883, 901 (1953)
(referring to Chief Justice Charles Evans Hughes)

As a pianist practises the piano, so the lawyer should practise the use of words, both in writing and by word of mouth.

Lord Denning, *The Discipline of Law* 7 (1979)

WORDPLAY

6.4 Hyperbole [hi-**pər**-bə-lee]: "overshooting." The use of exaggerated terms for the sake not of deception, but of emphasis, as when *infinite* is used for *great,* or *a thousand apologies* for *a single apology.*

[T]he Law of a great nation means the opinions of half-a-dozen old gentlemen . . . .

John Chipman Gray, *Nature and Sources of the Law*
84 (2d ed. 1921)

"They tell you at the Law School that the law is a wonderful science—the perfection of reason. Wonderful fiddlesticks! 'Tis in fact a hodge-podge of Roman Law, Bible texts, writings of the Christian fathers, Germanic customs, myths, canon law, superstitions, scraps of feudalism, crazy fictions, and long dead statutes. Your professors try to bring order out of chaos and make sense where the devil himself couldn't find any."

Caleb Tuckerman (as quoted in Ephraim Tutt,
Yankee Lawyer 41 (1943))

Lacking, perforce, any solid basis in precedent, vulnerable in theory and in logic, its central core of reasoning reversed within a week by another Court decision, *Marbury v. Madison* may seem scarcely worthy of the plaudits that have been heaped on it or the deference that has been paid it in the intervening century and a half. But both the plaudits and the deference, like the decision itself, and like every significant Supreme Court decision since, were and are rooted in politics, not in law. This only the ignorant would deny and only the naive deplore.

Fred Rodell, *Nine Men* 90 (1955)

[T]he awful fact is—according to the latest Rodell Random-Sample Poll—that 90 percent of American scholars and at least 99.44 per cent of American legal scholars not only do not know how to write simply; they do not know how to write.

Fred Rodell, *Goodbye to Law Reviews—Revisited,*
48 Va. L. Rev. 279, 288 (1962)

The judge who gives the right judgment while appearing not to do so may be thrice blessed in heaven, but on earth he is no use at all.

Patrick Devlin, *The Judge* 3 (1979)

6.5 Irony: "dissimulating." The use of words whose literal and figurative senses are opposites; that is, the difference between what seems to be said and what is meant. As the chief weapon of satirists, irony subverts the reader's expectations. A word of warning: law-review editors report that "most attempts by legal writers to employ irony ... range from ill-advised to pathetic."[6]

---

6. Jordan H. Leibman & James P. White, *How the Student-Edited Law Journals Make Their Publication Decisions,* 39 J. Legal Educ. 387, 423 (1989).

[T]he only thing about the appeals which we can commend is the hardihood in supposing that they could possibly succeed.

L. Hand, J., in *United States v. Minneci*,
142 F.2d 428, 429 (2d Cir. 1944)

Ownership meant no more to [the Shoshone Indians] than to roam the land as a great common, and to possess and enjoy it in the same way that they possessed and enjoyed sunlight and the west wind and the feel of spring in the air. Acquisitiveness, which develops a law of real property, is an accomplishment only of the "civilized."

Jackson, J., in *Northwestern Bands of Shoshone Indians*
v. United States, 324 U.S. 335, 357 (1945) (dissenting)

Where a man is fully occupied during the day, it is a heavy task for him to devote himself to the study of school subjects, with many of which, especially . . . Latin, he has but slight acquaintance, if any at all. Latin has been a sine qua non under the Law Society's regulations since 1938 . . . .

Glanville Williams (ed.), *The Reform of the Law* 36 (1951)

I cannot say that I know much about the law, having been far more interested in justice.

William Temple (former Archbishop of Canterbury)
(as quoted in Lord Denning's *The Road to Justice* 1 (1955))

[W]e hold that the first amendment does not clothe these plaintiffs with a constitutional right to sunbathe in the nude . . . . They remain able to advocate the benefits of nude sunbathing, albeit while fully dressed.

Henderson, J., in *South Fla. Free Beaches, Inc. v. City of Miami*,
734 F.2d 608, 610 (11th Cir. 1984)

In the last-quoted example, the irony occurs in the first sentence, the second containing mere tongue-in-cheek playfulness.

One of the most common types of irony is the Swiftian modest proposal, here executed with some success:

Of course, a simple mechanism for deterring violations such as [police brutality] would be to amend section 1983 to provide that violators will be drawn and quartered. This seems like a very powerful deterrent and might substantially reduce violations of federal rights under color of state law.

Goldberg, J., in *Dobson v. Camden*, 705 F.2d 759, 765 (5th Cir. 1983)

6.6 Meiosis [mɪ-**oh**-sis]: "lessening," and **litotes** [lɪ-tə-teez]: "frugality." The use of understatement not to deceive, but to enhance the impression on the hearer (e.g., "He is some judge."). When the figure takes the form of negating an opposite, it is called *litotes* (*not bad* [= good], *not guilty, not clearly erroneous*). The figure is often effective because the understatement may result in a quiet emphasis ("This is no anomaly"), or a humorous diminution ("He is no Clarence Darrow"). The first quotation below is emphatic, the second one diminutive:

> One who belongs to the most vilified and persecuted minority in history is not likely to be insensible to the freedoms guaranteed by our Constitution.
>
> Frankfurter, J., in *West Va. Bd. of Educ. v. Barnette,*
> 319 U.S. 624, 646 (1943) (dissenting)

> Although this history is absorbing, I do not find it a vade mecum.
>
> Henry Friendly, *The Fifth Amendment Tomorrow: The Case*
> *for Constitutional Change*, 37 U. Cin. L. Rev. 671, 678 (1968)

Beware the unappealing trick of writing *not un____*, a kind of litotes that convolutes lawyers' language. Swear off using it by saying to yourself, "A not unblack dog was chasing a not unsmall rabbit across a not ungreen field."[7]

6.7 Paronomasia [pa-ron-ə-**may**-zhə]: "punning, word-shunting." The jocular or suggestive use of similarity between different words or of a word's different senses. Puns seem increasingly popular in

---

7. George Orwell, *Politics and the English Language, in* 4 THE COLLECTED ESSAYS, JOURNALISM AND LETTERS OF GEORGE ORWELL 127, 138 n.1 (1968).

American legal prose. The ones found in titles to law-review articles are often delightfully clever. For example, the title of an article by Robert P. Mosteller, *Simplifying Subpoena Law: Taking the Fifth Amendment Seriously*,[8] plays effectively on two English idioms, *to take the Fifth Amendment* and *to take (something) seriously*.

Consider the title of a lawnote: *Designer Genes That Don't Fit: A Tort Regime for Commercial Releases of Genetic Engineering Products*, 100 Harv. L. Rev. 1086 (1987). The pun on *designer jeans* conveys the faddishness, or at least the currency, of genetic engineering. The strict regime offered, the title implies, will make genetic engineering fit into modern society, just as a good slimming diet is a virtual necessity for one who wants to wear designer jeans. In short, the pun works on two levels, though the comparison made by the pun is about as far-fetched as some of the conceits of John Donne, the great metaphysical poet.

Wrenching a legal cliché into an entirely fresh and literal application, one student titled his lawnote *Facial Discrimination: Extending Handicap Law to Employment Discrimination on the Basis of Physical Appearance*, 100 Harv. L. Rev. 2035 (1987). What a piquant and illuminating use of the phrase *facial discrimination*!

And of *sea change* here: Alan B. Sielen, *Sea Changes? Ocean Dumping and International Regulation*, 1 Georgetown Int'l Envtl. L. Rev. 1 (1988). The phrase *sea change* derives from Shakespeare's *The Tempest*, in which Ariel sings:

> Full fathom five thy father lies,
>   Of his bones are coral made:
> Those are pearls that were his eyes:
>   Nothing of him that doth fade,
> But doth suffer a sea-change
> Into something rich and strange.

> 1.2.400–05.

---

8.   73 VA. L. REV. 1 (1987).

The phrase came to denote any dramatic change for the better, originally one wrought by the sea (as the forming of a pearl). But in the title of Sielen's article, we see an allusive pun ironically used—for it is the sea that is being transformed, and for the worse.

Other punning titles abound nowadays, such as these:

Heidi Skuba Maretz, Note, *Aural Sex: Has Congress Gone Too Far by Going All the Way with Dial-a-Porn?*, 11 Hastings Comm. & Ent L.J. 493 (1989).

Michael B. Landau, *The Colorization of Black-and-White Motion Pictures: A Gray Area in the Law*, 22 Loy. L.A. L. Rev. 61 (1989).

Tracy N. Tool, Note, *The Luck of the Law: Allusions to Fortuity in Legal Discourse*, 102 Harv. L. Rev. 1862 (1989).

Note, *Begging to Defer: OSHA and the Problems of Interpretive Authority*, 73 Minn. L. Rev. 1336 (1989).

A strained yet clever pun occurred to the federal judge who wrote, "*Ticonic*'s cloth cannot be cut to fit Interfirst's suit."[9] Here *suit* carries the double sense, on the one hand, of completing the tailoring metaphor (cutting cloth for a suit) and, on the other hand, of denoting the lawsuit at issue.

But probably half the puns one sees in modern legal writing are the empty kind of wordplay in which one of the senses is inapposite or, worse yet, gibberish. For example, "The bells do not toll the statute of limitations while one ferrets out the facts." The pun here is on *toll*, which on the obvious level (*bells . . . toll*) means, nonsensically, "to ring"; the legal sense of *toll*, the one that gives meaning to the sentence, is "to abate." The pun in no way contributes to the sense. It's more likely to confuse or annoy than to enlighten.

As Charles Lamb observed, "A pun is not bound by the laws which limit nicer wit. It is a pistol let off at the ear; not a feather to

---

9. Interfirst Bank Abilene v. FDIC, 777 F.2d 1092, 1097 (5th Cir. 1985) (discussing Ticonic Nat'l Bank v. Sprague, 303 U.S. 406 (1938)).

tickle the intellect." Even so, in punning one must not abandon the intellect, for then one becomes a nuisance to the reader. Lamb also cautioned that puns sometimes show "much less wit than rudeness," adding: "We must take in the totality of time, place, and person."[10]

SYNTACTIC ARRANGEMENT

6.8 Anastrophe [ə-**nas**-trə-fee]: "turning back." This figure is also known as **hyperbaton** [hɪ-**pər**-bə-ton]: "stepping over." The inversion of the customary or logical order of words or phrases, especially for the sake of emphasis.

> A trustee is held to something stricter than the morals of the market place. Not honesty alone, but a punctilio of an honor the most sensitive, is then the standard of behavior.
>
> Cardozo, J., in *Meinhard v. Salmon*, 164 N.E. 545, 546 (N.Y. 1928)

> Rules we must have.
>
> Jerome Frank, *Courts on Trial* 411 (1949; repr. 1950)

> On the words you use, your client's future may depend.
>
> Lord Denning, *The Discipline of Law* 5 (1979)

> Constitutional choices must be made; to all of us belongs the challenge of making them wisely.
>
> Laurence H. Tribe, *Constitutional Choices* vii (1985)

Use this device sparingly if at all. Otherwise, you run the risk of sounding more like a mystic than a legal thinker.

6.9 Antithesis [an-**tith**-ə-sis]: "placing opposite." A choice or arrangement of words, often in parallel structure, that emphasizes a contrast. ("Crafty men contemn studies; simple men admire them; and wise men use them.") The contrast should always be be-

---

10. Charles Lamb, *Popular Fallacies*—. . . *That the Worst Puns Are the Best, in* ESSAYS OF ELIA AND LAST ESSAYS OF ELIA 306, 306–07, 308 (1906; repr. 1957).

tween ideas of the same order: one should not write, "Our efforts have been consolidated, not abandoned." The proper contrast to *consolidate* is *disperse*; and to *abandon, continue.* Also, avoid mixing metaphors: "Our resolve has not evaporated; it has deepened."

> If a business is unsuccessful it means that the public does not care enough for it to make it pay. If it is successful the public pays its expenses and something more.
>
> Holmes, J., in *Arizona Copper Co. v. Hammer,*
> 250 U.S. 400, 433 (1919) (concurring)

> Law must be stable and yet it cannot stand still.
>
> Roscoe Pound, *Interpretations of Legal History* 1 (1923)

> Legislation is something we must have; and yet admittedly it is most unsatisfactory in practice.
>
> Roscoe Pound, "The Task of the American Lawyer" (1925),
> in 6 *Modern Eloquence* 308, 321 (1928)

> By his public appearance and speech he would disclose himself as a temperate man or a violent one, a reasonable leader that well-disposed workmen could follow or an irresponsible one from whom they might expect disappointment, an earnest and understanding leader or a self-seeker.
>
> Jackson, J., in *Thomas v. Collins,*
> 323 U.S. 516, 546 (1945) (concurring)

> [A] fact is something perceptible by the senses, while law is an idea in the minds of men.
>
> Glanville Williams, *Criminal Law: The General Part* § 100,
> at 287 (2d ed. 1961)

In the following example, Justice Robert H. Jackson uses anastrophe (see 6.8) in tandem with antithesis:

> Very many are the interests which the state may protect against the practice of an occupation, very few are those it may assume to protect against the practice of propagandizing by speech or press.
>
> Jackson, J., in *Thomas v. Collins,*
> 323 U.S. 516, 545 (1945) (concurring)

6.10 Asyndeton [ə-**sin**-di-ton]: "not bound together." Purposeful omission of conjunctions that ordinarily join related words or clauses ("I came, I saw, I conquered"). (Cf. "Polysyndeton," 6.24.)

> There was the lack of agreement on the fundamental principles of the common law; lack of precision in the use of legal terms; conflicting and badly drawn statutory provisions; attempted distinction between cases where the facts present no distinction in the legal principles applicable; the great volume of recorded decisions; ignorance of judges and lawyers; the number and nature of novel legal questions.
>
> Benjamin N. Cardozo, *The Growth of the Law* 3–4 (1924)

> The allocation of power between nation and state is the pervasive problem of our federalism, *McCulloch* the most important case addressing that problem, Chief Justice Marshall's the most influential analysis.
>
> Gerald Gunther, *John Marshall's Defense of McCulloch v. Maryland* 2 (1969)

> Without the concrete instances the general proposition is baggage, impedimenta, stuff about the feet.
>
> Karl Llewellyn, *The Bramble Bush* 12 (1930; repr. 1951)

6.11 Climax: "ladder." Arrangement of a series of notions in such an order that each is more important or impressive than the preceding. Perhaps the most famous example is Caesar's sentence: *Veni, vidi, vici.* Often, as in the second example below, climax appears in a periodic sentence (see 6.13).

> Truth, like all other good things, may be loved unwisely—may be pursued too keenly—may cost too much.
>
> Vice-Chancellor Knight Bruce, in *Pearse v. Pearse* [1846] 1 De G. & Sm. 12, 28–29, 63 Eng. Rep. 950, 957

> If *Marbury v. Madison* was the most important decision in Supreme Court history and the Dred Scott case the most famous or infamous, if 1895 with its trio of triumphs over Congress was the Court's

biggest year from the standpoint of blatant judicial supremacy, still the most important and famous and exciting short-span period in the annals of the high tribunal, to date, was the three-year stretch from early 1935 through 1937 when the Justices clashed, head-on and eyes wide open, with Franklin Roosevelt's New Deal.

Fred Rodell, *Nine Men* 213 (1955)

A witty judge once said of the judicial life that the young judge spent the first third of it in fear that he might be reversed in the Court of Appeal, the middle third in the conviction that the Court of Appeal was always wrong, and the last third not caring whether it was right or wrong.

Patrick Devlin, *The Judge* 26 (1979)

The opposite of climax—anticlimax—is a common fault. For example, when you use adjectives together, end with the strongest, not the weakest.

For the accused to conduct these speculative land sales, always for his own profit, was vicious and unsound.

Most of us, of course, believe that any human conduct that is vicious is also unsound. The word *vicious* swallows the word *unsound*. If both must appear, then write:

For the accused to conduct these speculative land sales, always for his own profit, was unsound—even vicious.

6.12 Parallelism: "alongside one another." The use, for rhythmic effect, of similar constructions in adjacent syntactic units, often giving an equivalent, complementary, or antithetic sense. (See "Antithesis," 6.9.)

The Constitution of the United States is a law for rulers and people, equally in war and in peace, and covers with the shield of its protection all classes of men, at all times, and under all circumstances.

Davis, J., in *Ex parte Milligan*, 71 U.S. (4 Wall.) 2, 120–21 (1866)

So long as the leaders of the bar do nothing to make the materials of our legal tradition available for the needs of the twentieth century, and our legislative lawmakers, more zealous than well-instructed in the work they have to do, continue to justify the words of the chronicler—"the more they spake of law the more they did unlaw"—so long the public will seek refuge in specious projects of reforming the outward machinery of our legal order in the vain hope of curing its inward spirit.

> Roscoe Pound, "The Future of Legal Education," in *Indiana University, 1820–1920, Centennial Memorial Volume* 259, 268 (1921)

In tribal times, there were the medicine men. In the Middle Ages, there were the priests. Today there are the lawyers. For every age, a group of bright boys, learned in their trade and jealous of their learning, who blend technical competence with plain and fancy hocus-pocus to make themselves masters of their fellow men. For every age, a pseudo-intellectual autocracy, guarding the tricks of its trade from the uninitiated, and running, after its own pattern, the civilization of its day.

> Fred Rodell, *Woe Unto You, Lawyers!* 1 (1939; repr. 1980)

6.13 Periodic Sentence. A sentence consisting of a number of dependent clauses depending on a main clause at the end. Periodic sentences are of two types: those involving postponed predication and those involving suspended (or interrupted) predication. They have an Asiatic flavor (see Chapter 1), since they lead to a more complicated syntax than is usual.

a. Postponed Predication. This method builds tension as the principal assertion approaches. The main clause occurs entirely at the end of the sentence.

> Only when you have worked alone—when you have felt around you a black gulf of solitude more isolating than that which surrounds the dying man, and in hope and in despair have trusted to your own unshaken will—then only will you have achieved.
>
> Oliver Wendell Holmes, "The Profession of the Law,"
> in *Collected Legal Papers* 29, 32 (1920; repr. 1952)

When men and women disagree about whether the right of free speech extends to abusive language, or whether capital punishment is cruel and unusual within the meaning of the constitution, or whether a group of inconclusive precedents establishes a right to recover for merely economic damage in tort, then it is both silly and arrogant to pretend that there is somehow, latent in the controversy, a single right answer.

Ronald Dworkin, *Taking Rights Seriously* 279 (1977)

Judicial opinions deserve to be taken seriously. Only when we do take them seriously, when the profession insists that their authors hold themselves to standards as high as those by which the great composers, writers, and painters are content to have their work judged, will it be possible for some future Coen lecturer to consider judicial opinions as one of the fine arts without running the risk of being thought facetious.

Irving Younger, *On Judicial Opinions Considered as One of the Fine Arts*, 51 U. Colo. L. Rev. 341, 352–53 (1980)

Sometimes a sentence that shows all the early traits of postponing predication to its very end achieves closure before that point—as by adding another dependent clause at the end. In these cases, the periodic result is approximate, not strict.

When the very merits of the case are clear; when only one result can honestly emerge; and when the jury has in fact been satisfied, we no longer look upon criminal procedure as a sacred ritual, no part of which can be omitted without breaking the charm.

L. Hand, J., in *United States v. Brown*, 79 F.2d 321, 326 (2d Cir. 1935)

b. Suspended (or Interrupted) Predication. The difference between this method and the one just mentioned is that here the main clause begins early in the sentence but is interrupted by phrasal modifiers. The subject and the verb are typically parted by intervening words.

The mark of a master is that facts which before lay scattered in an inorganic mass, when he shoots through them the magnetic current of his thought, leap into an organic order, and live and bear fruit.

Oliver Wendell Holmes, "The Use of Law Schools," in *Collected Legal Papers* 35, 37 (1920; repr. 1952)

All that The Law is, all that it amounts to, all that it is made of, all that lawyers know and non-lawyers don't know, is a lot—a miscellaneous and tremendous lot—of abstract principles.

Fred Rodell, *Woe Unto You, Lawyers!* 109 (1939; repr. 1980)

Who could disagree that constitutional decisions—choices among competing constitutional arguments and meanings—ought to, and necessarily do, represent something less whimsical and personal than the unconstrained "will of the judges"?

Laurence H. Tribe, *Constitutional Choices* 3 (1985)

6.14 Rhetorical Question. A question put not to elicit information, but as a more striking substitute for a statement. As Fowler points out, "The assumption is that only one answer is possible, and that if the hearer is compelled to make it mentally himself it will impress him more than the speaker's statement."[11] Sometimes the writer supplies the answer at once, as in the second paragraphs of the first and third specimens.

Suppose the question of eating certain kinds of food or drinking certain kinds of liquid were put up to the community, and forty percent of the people thought it was right. Who are the other sixty percent who would have the audacity to send those forty percent to jail for doing something the sixty didn't believe in?

On how many questions do two people think alike? They can go only a certain way, when they branch off and leave each other.

Clarence Darrow, "Prohibition," in *Verdicts Out of Court* 106, 117 (1963)

---

11. H.W. Fowler, A Dictionary of Modern English Usage 616 (1926; repr. 1950).

The necessity for choosing collective bargaining representatives brings the same nature of problems to groups of organizing workmen that our representative democratic processes bring to the nation. Their smaller society, too, must choose between rival leaders and competing policies. This should not be an underground process. The union of which Thomas is the head was one of the choices offered to these workers, and to me it was in the best American tradition that they hired a hall and advertised a meeting, and that Thomas went there and publicly faced his labor constituents. How better could these men learn what they might be getting into?

Jackson, J., in Thomas v. Collins,
323 U.S. 516, 546 (1945) (concurring)

If the statute before us required labor union officers to forswear membership in the Republican Party, the Democratic Party or the Socialist Party, I suppose all agree that it would be unconstitutional. But why, if it is valid as to the Communist Party?

The answer, for me, is in the decisive differences between the Communist Party and every other party of any importance in the long experience of the United States with party government.

Jackson, J., in American Communications Ass'n v. Douds,
339 U.S. 382, 422 (1950) (concurring and dissenting)

Some rhetorical questions set forth the issue to be discussed at length. Ronald Dworkin frequently uses this device, as in titling his essays: "Is There Really No Right Answer in Hard Cases?" "Can a Liberal State Support Art?" "Is Wealth a Value?" "Do We Have a Right to Pornography?"[12] The device is often subtler than might appear at first glance. In his essay on pornography, for example, Dworkin begins: "It is an old problem for liberal theory how far people should have the right to do the wrong thing. Liberals insist that people have the legal right to say what they wish on matters of political or social controversy. But should they be free to incite racial hatred, for example?"[13]

---

12. These essays and 15 others appear in Dworkin's A MATTER OF PRINCIPLE (1985).
13. *Id.* at 335.

REPETITION

6.15 Alliteration [ə-lit-ə-**ray**-shən]: "letter-tagging." The noticeable or effective repetition of similar sounds, either in the vowels (assonance) or in the consonants (consonance). It may be used for a variety of effects. For example, Rodell achieves a pungency in the third of the examples next quoted by repeating the plosive *p*. Use this figure sparingly, for a special emphasis, as in these quotations.

> The life of the law has not been logic: it has been experience.
> Oliver Wendell Holmes, *The Common Law* 5 (1881; repr. 1963)

> Law is no longer thought of as something cabined and confined in a narrow compartment of its own to be opened only by the specialist.
> Benjamin N. Cardozo, "Modern Trends in the Study and Treatment of the Law" (1924), in 6 *Modern Eloquence* 34, 40–41 (1928)

> A quarter century has wrought no revolution among the professional purveyors of pretentious poppycock . . . .
> Fred Rodell, *Goodbye to Law Reviews—Revisited*, 48 Va. L. Rev. 279, 286 (1962)

Unconscious alliteration is usually a fault, as in the news item that read, "The guerrillas are re*port*ed to have seized this im*port*ant *port*, and reinforcements have been dispatched for sup*port*." But the clink of unconscious alliteration is often subtler than that. Here, for example, one sees no purpose behind the alliteration, which merely distracts:

> I am not writing for those who feel *con*fident that canons of appropriate *con*stitutional *con*struction may be *con*vincingly derived from some neutral source . . . .
> Laurence H. Tribe, *Constitutional Choices* 3 (1985)

6.16 Anadiplosis [an-ə-di-**ploh**-sis]: "doubling." Repetition of the last word, or any prominent word in a sentence or clause, at the beginning of the next, which begins an adjunct idea ("Reply on his honor—honor such as his?").

Fifty percent of all the cases that are brought to [a lawyer] are lost—
and must be lost, so long as law is what it is.
So long as law is what it is. Not, it may be, forever. For there is
nothing sacred, there is nothing immanent . . . .
Karl Llewellyn, The Bramble Bush 143 (1930; repr. 1951)

One difficulty that immediately confronts process theories is the
stubbornly substantive character of so many of the Constitution's
most crucial commitments: commitments defining the values that
we as a society, acting politically, must respect.
Laurence H. Tribe, Constitutional Choices 10 (1985)

The idea that the government should not interfere with freedom of
speech—should even protect it—has been with us only a few centuries. A few centuries is a brief period in all of history, and not till
the last of them has the kind of freedom that is the subject of this
book been at issue.
Charles Rembar, The End of Obscenity 11 (1968; repr. 1986)

6.17 Anaphora [ə-**naf**-ə-rə]: "bringing back." The marked repetition of a word or words at the beginning of two or more successive
clauses.

The melancholy and surprising feature of it all is not merely that
such things exist. The melancholy and surprising feature is that they
do not raise a ripple upon the placid surface of contentment.
Benjamin N. Cardozo, "Modern Trends in the Study and Treatment
of the Law" (1924), in 6 Modern Eloquence 34, 43 (1928)

The question whether a city-helped housing project may discrimi-
nate against a Negro war veteran (which split the top court of New
York state, four to three); the question whether a radio station is "ob-
structing justice" when it broadcasts a defendant's alleged out-of-
court confession during a murder trial (which pits one civil liberty
against another—the guarantee of a fair trial against the guarantee
of free speech and press); the question whether a fugitive from a
Georgia chain gang must be sent back from his hard-won asylum in
another state to what the Constitution calls "cruel and unusual punishment"; the question whether movies, like newspapers and books,

are protected from narrow local censorship by freedom of the press: all these questions and dozens like them, within the short space of two Court terms, were deemed by Vinson and company not worthy of decision—or perhaps too hot to handle.

Fred Rodell, *Nine Men* 15 (1955)

Every so often the Appeal Committee of the House of Lords produces a decision that sets back the rational development of the criminal law for several years or decades.

Other courts do this too. But when the lords are at fault it is particularly disappointing: because they should be the elite of the judiciary; because they have the time to consider their decisions properly; because counsel who argue cases before them (having thrashed them out in two lower courts) should be unusually well-prepared; because the lords have the authority to overrule ill-considered decisions of the lower courts; and because their own pronouncements are (if things go wrong) especially hard to overturn.

Glanville Williams, *The Logic of "Exceptions,"*
47 Cambridge L.J. 261, 261 (1988)

At the hands of Glanville Williams, the House of Lords as a court of final appeal takes a drubbing. But notice how this second paragraph could be tightened in its parallelism to intensify that drubbing. Making the final sentence a periodic one (see 6.13) heightens the reader's anticipation:

Other courts do this too. But because the lords are the elite of the judiciary; because they have the time to consider their decisions properly; because counsel who argue cases before them (having thrashed them out in two lower courts) should be unusually well prepared; because the lords have the authority to overrule ill-considered decisions of the lower courts; and because the lords' own pronouncements are (if things go wrong) especially hard to overturn, it is particularly disappointing when the lords are at fault.

6.18 Antanaclasis [an-tə-**nak**-lə-sis]: "bending back in the opposite direction." Repetition of a word in two different senses. (Cf.

"Paronomasia," 6.7.) Jesse Jackson provided a popular example in the late 1970s when he said, "Hands that picked cotton ten years ago are now picking presidents."

Other cases get distinguished and distinguished till they provoke the aphorism that a distinguished case is a case that is no longer distinguished.

Thomas R. Powell, *Some Apects of American Constitutional Law*, 53
Harv. L. Rev. 529, 537 (1940)

We can afford no liberties with liberty itself.

Jackson, J., in *United States v. Spector*,
343 U.S. 169, 180 (1952) (dissenting)

Marshall's Court ruled that the claims, though concededly conceived in fraud, were still perfectly valid and that the state of Georgia had to honor them. The get-rich-quick gamblers eventually collected close to five million dollars. U.S. law collected a new principle . . . .

Fred Rodell, *Nine Men* 101 (1955)

Etymologically . . . any depersonalized picture of a possible sexual partner represents the purest pornography you can get; how much more stimulating, though, is a real girl in a miniskirt. Women cannot help moving, and men cannot help being moved.

Anthony Burgess, "What Is Pornography?,"
in *Urgent Copy* 254, 255 (1968)

6.19 Chiasmus [kɪ-**az**-məs]: "cross-fashion." The repetition of words, in successive clauses, in reverse grammatical order. For example: "A juggler is a wit in things, and a wit is a juggler in words."

Jurisdiction exists that rights may be maintained. Rights are not maintained that jurisdiction may exist.

Cardozo, J., in *Berkovitz v. Arbib & Houlberg, Inc.*,
130 N.E. 288, 291 (N.Y. 1921)

The complementary concepts—that federal courts must follow state decisions on matters of substantive law appropriately cognizable by the states whereas state courts must follow federal decisions on subjects within national legislative power where Congress has so directed—seems so beautifully simple, and so simply beautiful, that we must wonder why a century and a half were needed to discover them . . . .

> Henry Friendly, *In Praise of Erie—and of the New Federal Common Law*, 39 N.Y.U. L. Rev. 383, 422 (1964)

[T]he rule follows where its reason leads; where the reason stops, there stops the rule.

> Karl Llewellyn, *The Bramble Bush* 157–58 (1930; repr. 1951)

We are not final because we are infallible, but we are infallible only because we are final.

> Jackson, J., in *Brown v. Allen*, 344 U.S. 443, 540 (1953) (concurring)

6.20 Epanalepsis [ep-ə-nə-**lep**-sis]: "taking up again." Repetition at the end of a clause of the word that began the clause.

The England that saw the birth of English law, the England of Magna Carta and the first parliaments, was a much governed and a little England.

> 1 Frederick Pollock & Frederic Maitland, *The History of English Law* 688 (2d ed. 1899)

The judge who administers law by means of "hunches" . . . is certain to be a very bad judge.

> Carlton K. Allen, *Law in the Making* 350–51 (7th ed. 1964)

The prostitute exploits the lust of her customers, and the customer the moral weakness of the prostitute.

> Patrick Devlin, *The Enforcement of Morals* 12 (1968)

In one of its old-fashioned forms, epanalepsis consists in repeating a word or phrase after intervening matter, as here:

"Speak not ill of a great enemy," says Selden in his *Table-Talk*—and Selden, you must know, was one of the ancient sages of our law— "speak not ill of a great enemy, but rather give him words that he may use you the better if you chance to fall into his hands . . . ."

> Benjamin N. Cardozo, "What Medicine Can Do for Law" (1928), in *Law and Literature and Other Essays and Addresses* 70, 71 (1931)

6.21 Epistrophe [ee-**pis**-trə-fee]: "turning around." Repetition of an expression at the end of successive phrases, clauses, or sentences.

It is rather for us to be here dedicated to the great task remaining before us; . . . that government of the people, by the people, and for the people, shall not perish from the earth.

Abraham Lincoln, "Gettysburg Address" (1863),
in Speeches and Letters 213–14 (1907; repr. 1940)

Eat law, talk law, think law, drink law, babble of law and judgments in your sleep. Pickle yourselves in law—it is your only hope.

Karl Llewellyn, The Bramble Bush 96 (1930; repr. 1951)

6.22 Epizeuxis [ep-i-**zook**-sis]: "yoking together." Emphatic and immediate repetition.

Everything, everything, everything, big or small, a judge may say in an opinion, is to be read with primary reference to the particular dispute, the particular question before him.

Karl Llewellyn, The Bramble Bush 43 (1930; repr. 1951)

With all due respect, the majority's new en banc basis for decision, though not as sweeping as its per se panel ruling, is still wrong, wrong, wrong.

Clark, C.J., in Affiliated Capital Corp. v. City of Houston,
741 F.2d 766, 767 (5th Cir. 1984) (dissenting)

[T]he furious building of prisons, the stiff laws, the cries for more, more, more in the way of punishment—what has the upshot been? The effect on crime: imperceptible.

Lawrence M. Friedman, Crime and Punishment
in American History 460 (1993)

We cannot allow losing to . . . frighten us from trying our next tough case. Otherwise, our value as lawyers and human beings is diminished. We must be willing to take the risk and try, try, try again.

J. Gary Gwilliam, The Art of Losing, Trial, May 1998, at 79, 79

6.23 Pleonasm [**plee**-ə-naz-əm]: "exceeding." This may denote either a fault or a grace. The term often means "redundancy" and is used disparagingly, but it also has a rhetorical sense in which it refers to purposeful amplification that clarifies or elaborates the thought. That is the sense here intended.

> Seen thus, perhaps, law appears to be a tiny thing, an infinitesimal part of civilization.
>
> Karl Llewellyn, *The Bramble Bush* 112 (1930; repr. 1951)

> When a court, then, fails wholeheartedly to enforce a statute, it sets itself against our constitutional scheme, acts undemocratically.
>
> Jerome Frank, *Courts on Trial* 292 (1950)

> The moderate stability of the judge-made rules, however, as I have already indicated, can be disrupted at any moment by the legislature. A statute—except in the few instances where it is unconstitutional— can change any judge-made rule.
>
> Jerome Frank, *Courts on Trial* 292 (1949; repr. 1950)

6.24 Polysyndeton [pol-ee-**sin**-də-ton]: "bound together." The repetition of conjunctions in close succession, as of *and* connecting coordinates or *or* connecting disjunctives. (Cf. "Asyndeton," 6.10.)

> [O]ur dead brother seemed to me too modest to be ambitious for reputation, and to regard his place mainly as an opportunity and a duty. He would have been most pleased, too, I dare say, to slip from it and from life, when his hour came without remark. He would have preferred not to be celebrated with guns and bells and pealing requiems, the flutter of flags and the gleam of steel in the streets, and all the pomp which properly is spent on those who have held power in their right hand.
>
> Oliver Wendell Holmes
> (paying tribute to William Allen in 1891), in *Speeches* 52, 54 (1934)

> My analysis of the judicial process comes then to this, and little more: logic, and history, and custom, and utility, and the accepted

standards of right conduct, are the forces which singly or in combination shape the progress of the law.

> Benjamin N. Cardozo, *The Nature of the Judicial Process* 112
> (1921; repr. 1968)

[T]he primitive man determines who shall prevail with sword and
club and tomahawk . . . .

> William L. Prosser, *The Law of Torts* § 3, at 15 (4th ed. 1971)

Justice Antonin Scalia has used polysyndeton in a mocking way to
show the endless variety of possibilities that he thought his colleagues had overlooked.

[A] particular legislator need not have voted for the Act either because he wanted to foster religion or because he wanted to improve
education. He may have thought that the bill would provide jobs
for his district, or may have wanted to make amends with a faction
of his party he had alienated on another vote, or he may have been
a close friend of the bill's sponsor, or he may have been repaying a
favor he owed the majority leader, or he may have hoped the Gov-
ernor would appreciate his vote and make a fundraising appearance for him, or he may have been pressured to vote for a bill he
disliked by a wealthy contributor or by a flood of constituent mail,
or he may have been seeking favorable publicity, or he may have
been reluctant to hurt the feelings of a loyal staff member who
worked on the bill, or he may have been mad at his wife who opposed the bill, or he may have been settling an old score with a legislator who opposed the bill, or he may have been intoxicated and
utterly unmotivated when the vote was called, or he may have acci-
dentally voted "yes" instead of "no," or, of course, he may have had
(and very likely did have) a combination of some of the above and
many other motivations.

> Scalia, J., in *Edwards v. Aguillard,*
> 482 U.S. 578, 637 (1987) (dissenting)

CONCLUSION

You've been exposed to rhetorical figures all your life. It's just that most of the time, you—like everyone else—didn't know it. Understanding how the choice and arrangement of words can increase their power requires alertness and quickness—and study. You needn't remember the names "anastrophe" and "epanalepsis" and the like; just remember that there are interesting, forceful ways to arrange words. You might occasionally review the examples in this chapter, and collect your own examples.

A 20th-century rhetorician emphasized the value of rhetoric by invoking the law's arbitrary-and-capricious standard: he said that when rules of rhetoric "are seen to be neither arbitrary nor capricious, but rational and logical, they may then cease to be irritating or boring."[14] He was right.

---

14. F.L. Lucas, *Style* 47 (1955; repr. 1962).

SEVEN

An Approach to Legal Style

Up to this point, we've been concerned with many of the minutiae of good writing. A good style depends on a command of them. But they're not enough. A writer must also internalize a number of broader principles, which are the subject of this chapter. Though stated in the imperative as "rules," these are intended more as gentle reminders.

BEING YOURSELF

7.1 Develop your own plain voice.

You are your style. If you're a novice who hasn't yet progressed to the point of having a distinctive style, the statement may seem unfair, just as it might be to say that your style indicates your character. In most legal writing, as it happens, the writer's personality gets suppressed.

But this isn't to say that you can write without a voice, any more than you can speak without one. Although your written voice might generally be subdued in legal prose, you can probably enliven your writing to good effect. The old advice for public speaking, "Just be yourself," holds equally true in writing. Try to express yourself honestly, clearly, unpretentiously. Your natural voice will emerge. As Arthur Quiller-Couch observed, "[T]he first and last secret of a good Style consists in thinking with the heart as well as with the head."[1]

What the head can do in legal writing is strive for a literate, precise, but relaxed style. Observe the voices of writers you admire, especially the good legal writers. You'll become aware of a broad range of possibilities in your own writing. But beware of giving your admiration too freely—without much critical thought—since whatever you admire in others' writing will affect your own.

What the heart can do in legal writing brings us to the next point.

7.2   When appropriate, invest your writing with some honest feeling.

Law is not just a bunch of dusty old precepts to be applied with humdrum objectivity. It is alive; blood courses through its veins. As often as not, to apply legal rules you must weigh, judge, and argue about human folkways and human foibles. And to do that well, you must have a heart.

Readers would probably be offended if briefs and judicial opinions about child custody, massive worker layoffs, abortion, or the death penalty completely ignored the human agony that these issues involve. For in the end, the law must serve justice.

Recognizing this fact is not a license to emote all over the page. But often in legal writing, sincerely expressing some feeling will work to your advantage. For example, the first Justice John Marshall Harlan showed magnanimity and empathy in his lone dissent in *Plessy v. Ferguson*, the case that gave rise to "separate but equal" facilities for blacks and whites:

> [T]he Constitution of the United States does not, I think, permit any public authority to know the race of those entitled to be protected in

---

1. ARTHUR QUILLER-COUCH, ON THE ART OF WRITING 291 (1916).

the enjoyment of such rights. Every true man has pride of race, and under appropriate circumstances, when the rights of others, his equals before the law, are not to be affected, it is his privilege to express such pride and to take such action based upon it as to him seems proper. But I deny that any legislative body or judicial tribunal may have regard to the race of citizens when the civil rights of those citizens are involved.

. . .

What can more certainly arouse race hate, what more certainly create and perpetuate a feeling of distrust between these races, than state enactments which in fact proceed on the ground that colored citizens are so inferior and degraded that they cannot be allowed to sit in public coaches occupied by white citizens?[2]

By contrast, Justice Henry B. Brown's majority opinion in *Plessy* shows what can happen when you write with your head but not your heart:

We consider the underlying fallacy of the plaintiff's argument to consist in the assumption that the enforced separation of the two races stamps the colored race with a badge of inferiority. If this be so, it is not by reason of anything found in the act, but solely because the colored race chooses to put that construction upon it.[3]

7.3   Establish your tone and stick to it.

The levels of diction in English are now less distinct than they once were, as reputable writers increasingly call on a wider spectrum of words to express themselves. Today most readers see no incongruity in using a word such as *trump* in the same sentence with *eminent domain*.

Even so, a slang phrase is probably inappropriate in an otherwise formal sentence because readers will sense a confusion of styles:

---

2. Plessy v. Ferguson, 163 U.S. 537, 554–55, 560 (1896).
3. *Id.* at 551.

This sort of Monday-morning quarterbacking not only encourages but almost compels the agency to conduct all rulemaking proceedings with the full panoply of procedural devices normally associated only with adjudicatory hearings.[4]

Your tone should vary with the topic. When the tone ill suits the subject matter, you leave readers befuddled:

> One bright sunshiny day in May 1918, while Katherine Veach was, with others, riding as a guest in an automobile from Louisville in the direction of Shelbyville, Ky., the machine was struck by an interurban electric car of appellee ..., and all five of the occupants of the automobile killed and the machine completely demolished.[5]

The opening phrase is reminiscent of a fairy tale, so the reader expects a light touch in what follows. But the writer then subverts that natural expectation. No doubt the judge's ironic purpose was to illustrate how Katherine Veach had set out cheerily with her friends, carefree and jovial, only to meet with a nightmarish end moments later. But tone by itself cannot achieve that effect. The better approach is to say directly what you mean. If your tone is light and cheery ("One bright and sunshiny day") and your subject is somber ("all five were killed"), the reader, taken unawares, may well think you a ghoulish writer.

Having a consistent tone doesn't mean allowing a pompous formality to petrify your prose. Nor must you eliminate all variety. What you want is a relaxed, comfortable tone. Judge Frank Easterbrook provides a good model:

> Arrested for feeding the pigeons and walking her dogs in the park, Anita Kirchoff recovered $25,000 from the police. The defendants gave up, but Kirchoff's lawyers did not. They wanted some $50,000 in fees under 42 U.S.C. § 1988. The district court gave them $10,000 on the ground that their contingent fee contract with the Kirchoffs

---

4. Vermont Yankee Nuclear Power Corp. v. Natural Res. Def. Council, Inc., 435 U.S. 519, 547 (1978).
5. Veach's Adm'r v. Louisville & Interurban Ry., 228 S.W. 35, 35 (Ky. 1921).

entitled them to 40% of any award. The case requires us to decide whether the contingent fee is the appropriate rate under § 1988 when the case resembles private tort litigation in which contingent fees are customary. First, however, we pause for the facts.[6]

Notice how, in the opening paragraph, Easterbrook covers a great deal of territory in a down-to-earth style. His first few words are not just interesting but startling. Then he synopsizes the litigation in a relaxed but confident tone: he uses everyday language, such as *gave up* (not *settled the litigation*), *gave them $10,000* (not *awarded to them a judgment in the principal amount of $10,000*), and the pronouns *they* and *them* (as opposed to repeating *the defendants*).

EXPOSITION AND ARGUMENT

7.4   Assume an audience of well-informed generalists.

Your readers may have legal training in common, but legal training can diverge greatly from one reader to the next. Unless you know otherwise, assume that your readers are generalists unversed in special technicalities. If you plunge straight into a complicated issue, you'll lose readers, however smart they may be. (They may be smart enough to quit on you, if you demand that they spend needless brainwork deducing your path.) Granted, you may be—had better be—an expert on what you're writing about. You're now well familiar, say, with the three criteria for successfully appealing an interlocutory order. Do you therefore begin by analyzing them?

No. Remember that your readers haven't been with you in your research. Even if they once knew the standards for taking an interlocutory appeal, you must jog the memory. Before launching into the analysis, briefly remind your readers of the fundamentals you intend to develop in the pages ahead.

But don't assume an audience of ignoramuses either. Readers

---

6. Kirchoff v. Flynn, 786 F.2d 320, 320 (7th Cir. 1986).

understandably resent the implication that they know nothing. For example, a law-review article in 1990 opened:

> In 1981, Justice (now Chief Justice) Rehnquist, concurring in Northern Pipeline, wrote . . . .

Can't we assume that readers of a law review will know who the current Chief Justice of the United States is? Even that they will know (more or less) when he ascended to that position? Most readers coming upon this reference will conclude that you have addressed someone else—an audience of tyros.

Even worse is the style in which writers define parties in the most pedantic way imaginable.

Not this:

Plaintiffs Lawrence Industries Inc. ("Lawrence") and Oriflamme Development Company ("Oriflamme") (collectively referred to herein as "Plaintiffs") move for a preliminary injunction enjoining Defendant Oliver Industries Inc. ("Oliver") from infringing U.S. Patent No. 4,850,120 (hereinafter "the '120 patent").

The qui tam action at issue here stems from a contract between Bulware Enterprises ("Bulware" or "the Company") and Eric Josephson ("Josephson" or "the Subcontractor") for the construction of subway tunnels beneath 44th Street and 43rd Street in New York City ("the City") ("Contract B-298-54"). Contract B-298-54 specified that Josephson would provide the Company with . . . .

But this:

Plaintiffs Lawrence Industries Inc. and Oriflamme Development Company move for a preliminary injunction to prevent Defendant Oliver Industries Inc. from infringing its '120 patent. [In the statement of facts, give the precise number of the patent when describing its issuance. Otherwise, refer to the '120 patent in the standard way.]

The qui tam action at issue here stems from a contract between Bulware Enterprises and Eric Josephson for the construction of subway tunnels beneath 44th Street and 43rd Street in New York City. Under the contract, Josephson was to provide Bulware with . . . .

Plaintiff Loftus Sugar, Inc. ("Loftus") moves for a temporary restraining order ("TRO") that would prevent Nathanate Crofters, Inc. ("NathCrofters") from violating a confidentiality and noncompetition agreement ("the Agreement").

Plaintiff Loftus Sugar, Inc. moves for a temporary restraining order that would prevent Nathanate Crofters, Inc. from violating a confidentiality and noncompetition agreement. [From this point, simply refer to Loftus, Nathanate, and the agreement—and perhaps use *TRO* (an abbreviation that every judge knows).]

For more on defined terms, see 4.5.

7.5 Sharpen your reasoning by summarizing your analysis up front, with just the amount of particularity that a generalist would need.

Whether you write a brief, an opinion letter, or a research memo—in fact, whenever you prepare any piece longer than one page—open with a summary. You'll actually *think* better when you do this. There are three parts to summarizing: the question, the answer, and the reason for the answer. (If you have several issues, of course, then the summary consists of questions, answers, and reasons.) Let's consider how these three parts show up in a good research memo.

First comes the most difficult part: the question. You must pose your question so that just about any reader will understand it on a first reading. This means that you must reject the four dogmas that have infected traditional thinking about issue-framing—namely, that you should (1) start with *Whether*, (2) put it into one sentence, (3) omit all facts, and (4) always make the question call for a "yes" answer. These dogmas lead to highly superficial issues, such as this:

Whether Mayor Frye is precluded from voting on Resolution 8308-01?

If those are the first words that a reader encounters, they're meaningless. And if they follow a long statement of facts, then the reader has had to plow through those facts without knowing what to look for. That is, the memo will resemble a law-school exam. Neither choice is much good.

But there's a better way: the deep issue. This means writing the question to enable all readers to understand it. The principles for a good deep issue—and you may have several deep issues in a given memo—are as follows:

- You must not try to cram everything into one sentence. Use separate sentences.
- You must hold each issue to 75 or fewer words. (Otherwise, you'll lose focus and readers will lose patience.)
- You must interweave facts into the issue—and keep them in chronological order.
- The last sentence, which ends with a question mark, must flow directly from what precedes it. But remember that everything in the 75-word statement makes up the issue.

If you master this technique—especially if you've already learned the stifling one-sentence format—you'll no doubt feel liberated.

Consider the *Whether*-issue quoted above: the one about Mayor Frye. When you use the deep-issue technique, the problem comes into sharp focus:

> The California Political Reform Act prohibits a public official from participating in a decision in which he or she has a material financial interest. Georgette Frye, the mayor of Monrovia, California, owns two office buildings in downtown Monrovia. The City Council is now considering a resolution to provide a new sewer system for the downtown area. Is Mayor Frye prohibited from voting on the resolution?

If you try stuffing all that into one sentence, you'll plunge immediately into obscurity.

What follows a good deep issue? Put the answer next, coupled with a reason. Then your summary will be complete. For example, the question posed just above might have the following answer:

> Yes. Frye is precluded from voting on the resolution. Although the project will benefit the general public, the City's appraisers have estimated that Frye's property values will increase 20%. The Monrovia City Charter requires its mayor to join in making decisions on projects that will benefit the general public, but she can cast only a tie-breaking vote. And although the Reform Act does not bar an official with a conflict of interest from carrying out legally required functions, it does expressly provide that casting a tie-breaking vote is not legally required participation.

It wouldn't be any good just to say yes or no or maybe. You must include the reason for your answer. And if the answer is maybe, you'll need to explain why the ultimate answer might go one way or the other. And then you should give your best estimate of which way the scales tip.

In a research memo, make your first-page summary a transparent window into your analysis. If you have two or more issues, give them headings. Make each issue a multisentence statement culminating in a question. Put an answer right after it. At a glance, a reader can glean the gist of a 20-page memo. The research will remain useful for a long time—to whoever may need to read it. It will efficiently yield up information.

Essentially the same technique applies to brief-writing. The only difference, typically, is that the issue nudges the reader toward an answer. In effect, a persuasive issue is a syllogism with three special characteristics: (1) a major premise consisting of a concise statement of law; (2) a specific, concrete minor premise; and (3) a conclusion phrased as a question. You can do all this within 75 words, as the following examples illustrate. The first is an international-law issue, the second a criminal-law issue, and the third a corporate issue:

> • The Iraq Sanctions Regulations prohibit the importation of goods in which the Government of Iraq has any interest—pres-

ent, future, or contingent. In February 2001, Pallasko Oil Traders imported oil that was once the property of Iraq, but that had changed hands in February 1992, when Iraq's interest in the oil terminated. Yet the U.S. Customs Service seized Pallasko's imported oil. Was the seizure authorized? [65 words]

- The Michigan Health Code makes it a crime for a nursing-home administrator not to report abuse or neglect of a patient to the Health Department. Evelyn Gray, a patient at the Fillmore Dawdey Nursing Home, was left unattended for 24 hours, crawled out of bed, fell, and broke her leg. Janice Bankhead, Dawdey's administrator, admits that she knew of but did not report this incident. Did Bankhead commit a crime under the Code? [74 words]

- Montana law prohibits a corporate director from taking advantage of a business opportunity that the corporation would normally undertake. Linda Burkhalter is a board member of Franklin Lumber Co., which sells lumber. In February 2001, she bought 100,000 feet of lumber at a private timber sale. She resold the lumber for a substantial profit without first offering the opportunity to Franklin. Did she breach her duties as a corporate director? [70 words]

How, you may wonder, does such an issue fit into a traditional motion or brief? The answer is simple and straightforward. But before considering it, we must reject the boring, nonsubstantive, formulaic openings of traditional motions—the ones that do nothing but rename the parties, name counsel, and repeat the titles of papers. For example: "Bilterburg Corporation ('Bilterburg'), by and through its attorneys of record, Samblitz, Tillman, Flynn & Susko ('SFTS'), 3300 First Biltmore Center, Suite 1753, 1050 Crown Pointe Parkway, N.E., Atlanta, Georgia 30303-4515, respectfully states unto the court as follows: . . . ." What follows are facts. Though common, this type of opener is an embarrassment. It says nothing of importance. It violates the most fundamental rule of writing—that your opening words are the most crucial ones. And it typically means that the writer is delaying or altogether dodging the issues.

So back to our question: how should the issue appear? Perhaps the cleanest way to lead into the issue is to say something like this:

- This motion presents the Court with two issues:
  - [75-word issue statement]
  - [75-word issue statement]

- In deciding this motion, the Court need address only two issues:
  - [75-word issue statement]
  - [75-word issue statement]

- The Court may dispose of this motion to dismiss by deciding a single issue:
  [75-word issue statement]

  If the Court answers that question in the affirmative, it need go no further. If, however, the Court decides that the answer to that question is no, the Court will then need to deal with three other issues:
  - [75-word issue statement]
  - [75-word issue statement]
  - [75-word issue statement]

The strategies are almost endless. But the common characteristic is that each one gives you a fast start. It's fresh. It's case-specific. It's immediately informative.

The opener, of course, won't carry the day on its own. It's a promise about what follows. In the middle, you must state the facts, elaborate the legal premises, show how the facts tie into those premises, and then explain why the suggested conclusion is the proper one. All this becomes easier—both for you and for your readers—once you've framed the issues on page one.

So remember the three parts of any good summary: one or more tangible questions, clear answers, and specific reasons for those answers. When you disclose these items at the outset, you'll find that your thinking has grown sharper.

7.6   Take pains to be thorough, and then distill the essence. Get to the point.

Late-19th-century judicial opinions suggest that the bane of legal writing in that era was the failure to distinguish what was merely interesting (and often not so interesting) from what was necessary to the conclusion. Though not quite so widespread today, the bane still flourishes.

Legal readers aren't typically seeking diversion. They want reasoning and persuasion.

Sometimes, of course, details fulfill this desire. For example, in a brief or opinion that attempts to justify imposing a death sentence, we often see graphic descriptions of the murder and what led up to it. The details may even grow lurid, but the reader is moved to understand just how heinous the crime was. The gore may not be strictly necessary to the disposition of the case, but it provides important rhetorical support for the logical argument.

Just as often, though, details serve no rhetorical purpose. We fail to distill when we describe the signing of a contract by stating the number of earlier drafts in the negotiations, the location of the signing, the people present, and the climatic conditions—all this when the event of signing is not at issue. A complete history misdirects by requiring the reader to do what the writer should have done: answer the question, "What is really important here?"

Consider the classic syllogism:

All men are mortal.
Socrates is a man.
Therefore, Socrates is mortal.

We don't need to know that Socrates is bald, or how old he is, or where he lives, or anything else. Legal argumentation should be syllogistic in this way, omitting everything that isn't directly helpful to understanding the problem.

This lean, direct style helps readers immensely. "[S]trike the jugular," wrote Holmes, "and let the rest go."[7] A dawdling writer

will be a deserted writer. When readers discern no forward movement—and are asked to march in place for a while or to amble
without direction—they lose all patience. Here, for example, we
have a strongly stated question followed by platitudes that fail to
advance an argument:

> How can the organized bar help in addressing the educational prob-
> lems facing this country? Note that the question is not put as to
> whether the organized bar should be involved. As lawyers, we are in-
> extricably bound to the rest of society. What happens to us as a na-
> tion not only has a profound effect on our clients, it also has a
> profound effect on the quality of our personal lives and those of our
> families. Clearly, the welfare of our family members and clients de-
> pends on matters beyond the confines of the law. Over and above the
> practical impact that issues may have on us, we must remember that
> lawyers are not just members of society; we have been, and remain
> today, leaders of that society. Just as our renewed emphasis on pro-
> fessionalism reminds us of our duty to look beyond the narrow in-
> terests of our clients to the broader interests of the legal system, so
> too must we make the maximum use of the privileged position we
> hold for the benefit of society.
>
> The legal profession is in an ideal position to act as both a catalyst
> and a facilitator of consensus. No other profession intersects with
> every aspect of our society. Lawyers sit on the boards of every corpo-
> ration and public interest group. Lawyers are part of the decision-
> making bodies of most government agencies. Lawyers are an integral
> part of every activity because the law is the one common thread that
> runs through every human endeavor. Because of this unique posi-
> tion of lawyers, the organized bar has the ability to take a leadership
> role in assisting the nation in addressing vital issues. The fact that
> these issues go beyond the areas of law and jurisprudence does not
> lessen our ability to have an impact. Our combined education and
> experience will enable the organized bar to provide intelligent and
> incisive comment and direction.

---

7. OLIVER WENDELL HOLMES, SPEECHES 77 (1934).

On and on it goes. The writer of these paragraphs lost sight of the stated goal. He found several ways to say what should have been left unsaid—that lawyers are leaders—but failed to move anywhere. The prose has stagnated.

Omit whatever doesn't move toward your target. If you have no clear target in mind, you have no business putting pen to paper. (The target, remember, differs from the path, which you may not have charted in every detail.) Consider just how much ground Ronald Dworkin swiftly covers in this paragraph:

> The Constitution is the fundamental law of the United States, and judges must enforce the law. On that simple and strong argument John Marshall built the institution of judicial review of legislation, an institution that is at once the pride and the enigma of American jurisprudence. The puzzle lies in this. Everyone agrees that the Constitution forbids certain forms of legislation to Congress and the state legislatures. But neither Supreme Court justices nor constitutional law experts nor ordinary citizens can agree about just what it does forbid, and the disagreement is most severe when the legislation in question is politically most controversial and divisive. It therefore appears that these justices exercise a veto over the politics of the nation, forbidding the people to reach decisions which they, a tiny number of appointees for life, think wrong. How can this be reconciled with democracy? But what is the alternative, except abdicating the power Marshall declared? That power is now so fixed in our constitutional system that abdication would be more destructive of consensus, more a defeat for cultivated expectation, than simply going on as before. We seem caught in a dilemma defined by the contradiction between democracy and ancient, fundamental, and uncertain law, each of which is central to our sense of traditions. What is to be done?[8]

In some minor particulars, of course, the reader may be disappointed: Dworkin uses the *neither . . . nor* construction with three

---

8. Ronald Dworkin, *The Forum of Principle, in* A MATTER OF PRINCIPLE 33, 33 (1985).

elements (see 3.5, at pp. 71–73), uses *which* for *that* (see pp. 142–43), and twice relies on *this* to refer to a series of sentences (see pp. 143–44). But how swiftly he gets to his point, how deftly he propels the argument forward!

SPEAKING LEGALLY

7.7   Avoid jargon and beware terms of art.

When you find your writing "encrusted by the barnacles of jargon,"[9] don't rejoice at your acquisition of the briny mementos. Scrape away every trace of them if you can. In legal writing, jargon consists mostly of stilted words and phrases—blemishes, not graces—such as *aforesaid, arguendo, said* (as an adjective), *hereinafter, hereunto, before-mentioned, comes now, further affiant sayeth not, et ux., instanter, such* (person), *wherefore, to wit, witnesseth.* Most hoary legal phrases have little or no substantive purpose. They sometimes mar the substance by suggesting precision where in fact an ambiguity lurks. The only reason for using them is to affect a legalistic style—a style better interred than exhumed.

Good legal writing is hardly more than literary English applied to the subject of law. If we foster differences, we ought to know the reasons for those differences. We should question even such jargon as *the instant case* and *the case at bar.* Why not *this case* or even *here?* Most of the circumlocutions, formal words, and archaisms that characterize lawyers' speech and writing are easily simplified to good effect.

Not this:	*But this:*
abutting	next to
adequate number of	enough
anterior to	before

---

9. Continental Oil Co. v. Bonanza Corp., 677 F.2d 455, 460 (5th Cir. 1982).

at the present time	now
at the time when	when
by means of	by
cause X to be done	have X done, effect X
contiguous to	next to
divers	several, various
during such time as	while, as long as
excessive number of	too many
for the duration of	during
for the reason that	because
in case	if
in order to	to
instant (adj.)	this
in the event that	if
in the interest of	for
is able to	can
is entitled to (do)	may (do)
it is directed that	must
it is the duty of	must
notwithstanding the fact that	although
on grounds that, on the ground that	because
on or about	on, about (decide which applies)
period of time	period, time
previous to	before
prior to	before
pursuant to	under, in accordance with
subsequent to	after
sufficient number of	enough
the reason being that	because
until such time as	until

As a cynical wag once quipped, a lawyer would probably have titled Kipling's famous poem "In the Event That."

As for terms of art—legal terms with a specific meaning—these much-vaunted favorites are an endangered species. No longer must a testator use the formula *and his heirs* to create a fee simple.

Legal formalism continues its slow death. Most "lawyerly words" are mere legaldegook that can be translated, with precision, into plain English. Though we have hundreds of jargonistic terms, the common terms of art number fewer than a hundred. Count them: *plaintiff, defendant, fee simple, mandamus, mens rea, in rem,* and the like. Many supposed terms of art are too imprecise to be properly so classed: *ratio decidendi* and *res judicata* have more than one layer of meaning; so do *common law* and *equity* (many more layers). Because each of these terms spans an array of senses, you should specify the sense in which you use it.

Yet jargon may suit your purpose now and then. You may want to say *gift causa mortis* instead of *gift given by reason of the donor's immediate perception that he or she was dying.* Given the need to express the idea repeatedly, *gift causa mortis* grows on you quickly.

But never assume that traditional legal expressions are legally necessary. As often as not they are scars left by the law's verbal elephantiasis, which only lately has started into remission. Use words and phrases that you know to be both precise and as widely understood as possible. Rarely can you justify the little-known word on grounds that it is a term of art.

7.8   Write in English.

You should avoid Latin and French. This has at least three advantages. First, you'll succeed in communicating. No one benefits from a conclusion stated in this way:

> *Parens patriae* cannot be *ad fundandam jurisdictionem.* The zoning question is *res inter alios acta.*[10]

Second, you'll constrict that "marvelous capacity of a Latin phrase to serve as a substitute for reasoning."[11] Third, you won't embarrass

---

10. Mississippi Bluff Motel Inc. v. County of Rock Island, 420 N.E.2d 748, 751 (Ill. App. Ct. 1981).
11. Edmund M. Morgan, *A Suggested Classification of Utterances Admissible as Res Gestae,* 31 Yale L.J. 229, 229 (1922).

yourself with a pretentious blunder, as by writing *corpus delecti* in place of the correct phrase, *corpus delicti*: you'll neither show yourself to be a lack-Latin nor unwittingly arouse necrophiliacs.

The English language has fully naturalized dozens of Latin and French words and phrases: *a priori, bonus, cause célèbre, de facto, ex cathedra, vis-à-vis,* and so on. We have a number residing only in the legal domain: *de minimis, ex parte, habeas corpus, nolo contendere, prima facie, voir dire.* Several reside comfortably both in legal English and in the broader language: *alibi, bona fide, quorum.* What these phrases have in common is that they have each filled a gap in the English language.

Many foreignisms found in legal writing don't fill such gaps and haven't truly been imported into the English language. Why does anyone write that it would be *contra bonos mores* not to punish parents who fail to care for their children; that clauses to safeguard a party are included in contracts *ex abundanti cautela*; that an interest in realty begins *in praesenti,* or *in futuro*; that one undertakes to rescue another *sub suo periculo*? These terms convey no special legal meanings, no delicate nuances apprehended only by lawyers. They're pompous that have ready English equivalents.

Imported jargon accounts for much of the obscure lawyerly tongue, which excludes all but those initiated into the legal fraternity. Simplify wherever possible.

Not this:	*But this:*
ab initio	from the beginning
arguendo	for the sake of argument
cestui que trust	beneficiary
child en ventre sa mere	fetus, unborn child
ex contractu	in contract, contractual
ex delicto	in tort
ex hypothesi	by hypothesis, hypothetically
in esse	in being
in foro conscientiae	in the forum of conscience
in haec verba	verbatim, in these words

instanter	instantly
inter alia	among others
ipsissima verba	the very same words
non compos mentis	insane
res nova	undecided question, case of first impression
simpliciter	simply, summarily, taken alone
stricti juris	of the strict right of law
sui generis	one of a kind, unique
vel non	or not, or the lack of (it, them)

Before putting such words on paper, question your own motives. Are you really expressing yourself, or are you just trying to impress someone?

Our genuine dilemmas under this heading are few: whether to write *gift causa mortis* (see 7.7); whether to use the journalists' phrase *friend of the court* instead of *amicus curiae*; whether to write *doctrine of precedent* instead of *stare decisis*; *on its own motion* instead of *sua sponte*; and so on. Since lay readers have no better idea of what a *friend of the court* is than an *amicus curiae*—indeed, are more likely to believe mistakenly that they understand the English phrase—we hardly advance the principle of clear expression by adopting the journalists' phrase. In general, though, the best course is to use a native English expression if one is available and to use a foreignism only as a last resort. Rarely, we might say, is a foreignism the *mot juste*.

7.9   Instead of using doublets or triplets, use a single word.

Among the lawyer's least endearing habits is stringing out near-synonyms. The causes are several. First, the language of the law has its origins in the unhurried prose of centuries past. Second, the strong oral tradition in England led inevitably to a surfeit of words to allow time for the listener to take in the speaker's point. Third, if a word might be unfamiliar, the synonym served as a gloss. Finally, lawyers distrusted their ability to find the right word, and therefore used a verbal scattergun instead of a rifle. As a result, we still use phrases such as these:

> agree and covenant
> all and singular
> any and all
> bind and obligate
> cancel, annul, and set aside
> cease and desist
> do and perform
> due and payable
> give, devise, and bequeath
> indemnify and hold harmless
> liens and encumbrances
> null and void
> ordain and establish
> pay, satisfy, and discharge
> possession, custody, and control
> premeditation and malice aforethought
> remise, release, and forever quitclaim
> rest, residue, and remainder
> right, title, and interest
> uncontroverted and uncontradicted
> vague, nonspecific, and indefinite

That last string ties up nicely the main objection to these lawyerly word lists: they show no effort to be precise, specific, and definite. In a string such as *cancel, annul,* and *set aside,* any one of the three synonyms would suffice. In others, such as *possession, custody,* and *control,* one of the words is broad enough (*possession*) to swallow the others in most contexts. Very few such phrases—notably *aid and abet*—are necessary as terms of art. Unless you are certain that each additional word colors the sense as you desire—or unless you want a ceremonious tone (*the truth, the whole truth* . . .)—settle on the single most appropriate word.

7.10 Understate rather than overstate.

Writers too often cheapen words by inflating their value. When readers catch on, they intuitively adjust for the overstatement by believing a little less than what the writer has said, if indeed they believe any of it.

Unmindful of how judges are persuaded, advocates all too commonly try to reduce every argument of an opponent to "an utter fallacy," "a logical absurdity," or "an argument completely unsupported in law or in fact." Lawyers who adopt this approach seem to want every argument to be a knockout. They launch roundhouse punches at every turn. Judges quickly grow weary of refereeing these contests because they know that the world is more complicated than the belligerents would have it. Most cases have some merit on both sides; not every opposing argument can or need be pummeled down to absurdity.

Most issues about which serious argument takes place cannot be reduced to a simple dichotomy of right and wrong. Even in retrospect, after your side has won and the other has lost in court, you shouldn't think in these terms, since your client may have prevailed by a slight preponderance.

Take a measured, responsible approach in arguing against an opponent. Evaluate the other side's argument by attempting first to understand it. That advice sounds elementary, but lawyers frequently argue without truly understanding what their opponents are saying. Before rebutting the opposing arguments, try to state them as if you were the proponent. When you can do that, you can begin dismantling those arguments.

Successful written argument, then, does not take the most extreme possible position by grossly overstating the merits of one side and ignoring the merits of the other. Instead, it takes a more thoughtful approach. It refrains from exaggeration, from sweeping assertions that repel (not engage) the reader.

On the mundane level, "three" does not become "many"; a dog that has bitten a client's leg in self-defense does not become a "ferocious beast"; and corporate officers in a shareholder's derivative suit don't become "self-seeking moguls whose sole aim was to perpetuate themselves in office, whatever havoc they wreaked on the corporation." That's the type of writing that gave rhetoric a bad name.

EXPRESSIVE TACTICS

7.11 Put the action into verbs, not nouns and adjectives.

All too often, legal writers use phrases containing long nouns—especially nouns ending in -*ion*—to convey the same information as a simple verb. That is, some people write *submit an application* instead of *apply*, or *provide an indemnification to* instead of *indemnify*. There are countless other examples.

Not this:	But this:
enter into a compromise and settlement agreement	settle
exhibit resistance	resist
file a dissenting opinion	dissent
file a motion	move
focus criticism on	criticize
make a decision	decide
make an inquiry	inquire, ask
make reference to	refer to
offer a rebuttal	rebut
perfect an appeal	appeal
proffer an argument	argue
reach a resolution	resolve
show deference	defer
sign a contract (with)	contract (with)
take into consideration	consider

More than any other part of speech, verbs bring prose to life, or life to prose. But only action verbs do this—verbs such as *snatch, stop, grasp, run, urge.* Many English verbs, most notably forms of *be* (*is, are, might be,* etc.), are nondescript: they convey little if any action.

A *be*-verb functioning as part of a verb phrase often signals roundabout wording. For example, *be determinative of* is verbose for *determine.* This type of verbosity abounds in legal writing.

Not this:	*But this:*
be abusive of	abuse
be amendatory of	amend
be benefited by	benefit from
be decisive of	decide
be derived from	derive from
be desirous of	desire, want
be dispositive of	dispose of
be in agreement	agree
be in attendance	attend
be indicative of	indicate
be in dispute over	dispute, disagree
be in existence	exist
be influential on	influence
be in receipt of	have received
be in the exercise of due care	exercise due care
be possessed of	possess, have
be probative of	prove
be productive of	produce
be promotive of	promote
be violative of	violate

Many other wordy constructions can be boiled down to the present-tense singular: *is able to* (*can*), *is authorized to* (*may*), *is binding upon* (*binds*), *is empowered to* (*may*), *is required to* (*shall, must*), *is unable to* (*cannot* or *may not*).

Just as we say ¼ instead of ¹²⁄₄₈—when there is no reason for working with the larger denominator—so we should reduce our words to the kernel.

7.12 Stress nouns and verbs, not qualifiers.

Adjectives often weaken nouns, and adverbs often weaken verbs. Think of the best single word instead of warming up a tepid one with a qualifier. For example:

Not this:	*But this:*
She was extremely interested in the book.	She was enthralled by the book.
The customers were quite frightened by the gunman.	The customers were terrified by the gunman.

And be wary of the qualifiers that douse the statements they qualify: *somewhat, virtually, rather, surely.* Even would-be fortifiers such as *clearly, quite, undoubtedly,* and *undeniably* usually betray us (see 2.18).

When adjectives are placed in high relief, they sometimes serve us well. See what Clarence Darrow does with *selfish, superstitious, bigoted,* and *outrageous* here:

> He speaks of the people in the United States now as if they owned this country. Why, the first of them came over on the Mayflower. They couldn't stay at home without going to jail for debt. They were selfish, superstitious, and bigoted in the extreme. They came over here to get a chance. The real American was the Indian, and they solved that problem by killing him. The land was occupied, but they took it, and then our Puritan fathers proceeded to pass the most outrageous laws that any country ever knew anything about.[12]

Even so, the verbs and nouns do most of the work here, not the adjectives. If we qualify the passage with more adjectives and adverbs, it collapses into fecklessness:

---

12. Clarence Darrow, *The Immigration Law, in* Verdicts Out of Court 134, 137–38 (1963).

He speaks of the people in the United States now as if they *virtually* owned this country. Why, *many of* the first of them came over on the Mayflower. They couldn't, *for the most part,* stay at home without going to jail for debt. They were *extremely* selfish, *excessively* superstitious, and *quite* bigoted. They came over here *truly* to get a chance. The real American was the Indian, and they solved that *difficult* problem *more or less* by killing him. The land was *largely* occupied, but they *unashamedly* took it, and then our Puritan fathers proceeded *swiftly* to pass the *seemingly* most outrageous laws that *almost* any country ever knew anything about.

For their force, the two passages can hardly be compared. The second passage we know to be travesty. But any lawyer can attest to how these and other qualifiers pervade court papers, letters, judicial opinions, and law-review articles.

7.13 Mind the cadence of your prose.

Prose writers are seldom as sensitive to rhythm as poets, no doubt because rhythm is less crucial in prose. But it's still important. Rhythm makes the difference between clumsy, monotonous writing and graceful, logical writing. Masterly writing suggests inevitability—that no other placement of words, sentences, and paragraphs would have worked as well.

Overlook sentence length at your peril. Try to write mostly short sentences, but give some variety with an occasional long sentence. Ronald Dworkin provides a good example:

> These are the direct effects of a lawsuit on the parties and their dependents. In Britain and America, among other places, judicial decisions affect a great many other people as well, because the law often becomes what judges say it is. The decisions of the United States Supreme Court, for example, are famously important in this way. That Court has the power to overrule even the most deliberate and popular decisions of other departments of government if it believes they are contrary to the Constitution, and it therefore has the last word on whether and how the states may execute murderers or pro-

hibit abortions or require prayers in the public schools, on whether Congress can draft soldiers to fight a war or force a president to make public the secrets of his office.[13]

Apart from length, be sure that not every sentence follows the same structure. Once you have learned to vary the structure of your sentences, your rhythmic repertoire broadens to serve a greater variety of needs.

Strive for the best possible phrasing of your sentences. Just as a flutist must know when to take breaths without interrupting the flow of the music, you must consider where the pauses fall, and with what effect. Try reading this sentence aloud:

> The plaintiff having conveyed away by deed, purporting to grant a fee simple interest in the lands in question, and having had them conveyed back to her, is now seised of a fee simple interest.

We may question the wisdom of using a periodic sentence (see 6.13) for such a statement. But if we are to stay with that structure, we greatly improve the cadence by repositioning the subject directly before the verb and by making the participial phrase introductory:

> Having purported to convey a fee simple interest in the lands, and having had them conveyed back to her, the plaintiff is now seised of a fee simple interest.

Now let us depart from the periodic sentence:

> The plaintiff conveyed a fee simple interest in the lands and then had them conveyed back to her. So she now owns the lands in fee simple.

That's not moving prose, to be sure; but it is simple, clear, and tailored to the message. Why, for example, use the verb *purport* if we're conceding that the grant was effective?

Why indeed do we insert so many needless words? The result is awkward prose that lumbers along. One more example:

> The basis for, and the need of, such encouragement is no longer existent.

---

13. RONALD DWORKIN, LAW'S EMPIRE 2 (1986).

When we reduce the sentence from 13 to 8 words—partly by recognizing that the word *need* covers *basis*, as here used—we gain a more natural rhythm:

> The need for such encouragement no longer exists.

Or, if the meaning permits, six words:

> They no longer need such encouragement.

Paring down sentences in this way—cutting every word that does not directly advance the argument—almost always improves rhythm.

7.14 Use clichés with caution. And avoid purple prose.

Clichés are timeworn expressions, those once clever phrases that have been reduced to formula. The best way to handle clichés is not to avoid them altogether, but to use them warily. Usually a cliché (*comparing apples and oranges*) is better than a circumlocution invented merely to displace it (*comparing plums and pomegranates*). But avoid the prepared wads of verbiage that displace thought.

Good writers use clichés consciously, for a purpose. For example, a clever judge once wrote that the "unwritten law is not worth the paper it isn't written on." For a less waggish example, who doubts that Fred Rodell had the mountain-out-of-a-molehill cliché well in hand here?

> With law as the only alternative to force as a means of solving the myriad problems of the world, it seems to me that the articulate among the clan of lawyers might, in their writings, be more pointedly aware of those problems, might recognize that the use of law to help toward their solution is the only excuse for the law's existence, instead of blithely continuing to make mountain after mountain out of tiresome, technical molehills.[14]

---

14. Fred Rodell, *Goodbye to Law Reviews—Revisited*, 48 Va. L. Rev. 279, 284 (1962).

Contrast the seeming virtuosity of Rodell's phrasing with the almost oblivious use of a cliché at the end of this passage: "[A] recurrent dream of social reformers has been that the law should be (and can be) simplified and purified in such a way that the class of lawyers can be done away with. The dream has never withstood the cold light of waking reality."[15] One reads that last sentence with a sunken feeling.

Before using clichés such as these, make them prove themselves:

add insult to injury
all things considered
at first blush
back to the drawing board
blissful ignorance
by the same token
chilling effect
clean slate (we do not write on a, etc.)
commune with nature
considered opinion
constrained to hold
deliberate falsehood
distinction without a difference
eminently qualified
exercise in futility
fall on deaf ears
fateful day
foregone conclusion
form over substance
frame of reference
from the sublime to the ridiculous
garden-variety (case, etc.)
grievous error
in the same boat
it goes without saying
just deserts
keep (one's) options open

<hr>

15. GRANT GILMORE, THE AGES OF AMERICAN LAW 1 (1977).

landmark case
last-ditch effort
left up in the air
lock, stock, and barrel
matter of life and death
moment of truth
momentous decision
nip in the bud
none the wiser
no uncertain terms
no-win situation
one and the same
open and shut
paramount importance
part and parcel
powers that be
pros and cons
pull no punches
pure and simple
remedy the situation
Scylla and Charybdis, between
search far and wide
seat of justice
six of one, half a dozen of the other
sum and substance
sweeping changes
take up cudgels
there's the rub
throw the baby out with the bathwater
tide of battle
tides of time
trials and tribulations
unimpeachable integrity (or authority)
viable alternative
wait-and-see attitude
wheels of justice
woefully inadequate
wreak havoc

The list is not intended as one of forbidden phrases. Rather, when you find yourself about to use such a phrase, rethink what you want to say. How can you say it best? If you believe it is by consciously using a cliché, read the sentence and then the paragraph to yourself, listening especially for a tone of banality. You'll find that you use fewer clichés and achieve better results.

A related problem is purple prose: showiness that occurs when writers delight too much in their words and subordinate the message to their way of expressing it. Though hardly pervasive in legal writing, the problem is common enough to merit admonition. Out-of-hand metaphors jumble images: "[P]etitioner's asseveration, when *unrolled, embodied* evidence so *sparse,* a *pyramiding* of inferences so *fragile,* a thesis so speculative, as to *envelop* the bias/misconduct charge in a *miasma* of doubt."[16] Even the consistent metaphor—unmixed and perhaps allusive—can be made too fanciful:

> [U]nfortunately, the use conflicted in some points, not only with the eternal policy of the law, but also with the empirical policy of feudalism, and to end these conflicts a disastrous remedy was found. For the use was made to enter the Valley of Humiliation, goaded by the two-pronged fork wielded by Henry VIII, on one prong of which he had impaled the landowners, and on the other the lawyers, the two classes most friendly to the preservation of the use. The name of that valley was the Statute of Uses, and amidst the horrors of that valley we wandered for nearly 400 years. We have at last emerged, guided by the torch of the Earl of Birkenhead, but the baleful murk of the statute still encompasses old titles to land, which will continue to occupy the attention of the Courts for some time to come.[17]

Purple prose—"no substitute for relevance,"[18] as one court put it— results from overindulging one's imagination. Figures of speech

---

16. Neron v. Tierney, 841 F.2d 1197, 1203 (1st Cir. 1988).
17. H.G. HANBURY, MODERN EQUITY 7 (3d ed. 1943) (with acknowledgments to Robert E. Megarry's penetrating review of the book at 60 Law Q. Rev. 87, 92 (1944)).
18. Look Magazine Enters. S.A. v. Look, Inc., 596 F. Supp. 774, 779 (D. Del. 1984).

can be extremely effective, but only when used sparingly. Consider how differently the passage just quoted reads from the personifications of law quoted at 6.2; Holmes and Rodell control their metaphors, whereas Hanbury, the author of the preceding quotation, has let the metaphor run wild.

7.15 Root out sexist language.

Gender-neutral language isn't about political correctness; it's about credibility. Regardless of how you may feel about the old "rule" that the masculine *he* includes the feminine *she*—whether you detest it or you like it—you'll need to handle the English language with some care to have credibility with a wide range of readers.

This isn't an easy task. On the one hand, readers such as William Safire will think you're crazy if you write *he/she, s/he,* or *(s)he.* They'll know you're crazy if you write—as one book author has—the onomatopoeic symbol *s/he/it.* On the other hand, readers such as Susan Estrich will think you're a troglodyte if you use *he* to refer to readers generally—as if the feminine were the unstated exception swept into the masculine rule of our language.

Is there no way to win over your readers, then?

Yes, there is. It takes some skill and a lot of effort. With those two things, you'll be able to produce a style that never induces readers to consider your personal biases. If your point is that you *want* to induce this reaction, then you're rebuffing some of your readers—something you may willingly do unless you have a client whose money and perhaps even freedom are on the line. If you're trying to persuade someone on a point unrelated to sexist language, then the issue shouldn't even arise.

Perhaps every reader of this book already has opinions on the issue of sexist language. Whatever you may think, here are four points to ponder.

First, remember that readers come first—and there are many types. Don't stereotype your readers. Never assume that women are the only ones who care about sexism, or even that most women feel the same way about it. Though I'm a man, I happen to be distracted by sexist language. I'm not impressed with a book whose opening words are "For the lawyer more than for most men . . ."[19] —especially when warnings about sexist language appear fore and aft.[20]

And Chief Judge Judith Kaye, of the highest tribunal in the State of New York, is not alone when she declares: "I believe that gendered writing . . . will one day be immediately recognized as archaic and ludicrous."[21]

Second, pronouns aren't the only pitfall. One insidious type of sexism is the disparate ways of referring to men and women. Some will give prominent men their titles (*Secretary of State Colin Powell*) and then refer to prominent women in less exalted terms (*Condoleezza Rice* or *Ms. Rice* instead of *National Security Adviser Condoleezza Rice*). Or they'll give a male writer just the last name (*Llewellyn*) while repeatedly giving the full name of a woman (*Soia Mentschikoff*) or a sex-specific honorific (*Ms. Mentschikoff*). Some will call these imagined slights. But the disparities, even if unconscious, are hard to dismiss.

Third, keep your sense of what is good English. Remember the importance of tone—how you sound. Although it might be okay to use *he* or *she* once every few pages, you don't want to begin doing it at every turn. (Try pluralizing.) Write so that your prose is natural, even speakable. The whole idea is to avoid having readers think about your words when you're trying to get them to focus on what you're saying.

Fourth, monitor what's happening to the language. It's changing. A living language always does that—sometimes for better and sometimes for worse. In the end, most losses end up being gains as well.

---

19. HENRY WEIHOFEN, LEGAL WRITING STYLE 1 (2d ed 1980).
20. *Id.* at vii, 19.
21. Chief Judge Judith S. Kaye, *A Brief for Gender-Neutral Brief-Writing*, N.Y.L.J., 21 Mar. 1991, at 2.

Despite our considerable progress, writers must grapple with particular problems in wording. There are many ways to avoid sex-specific pronoun references. Consider any of the choices below, but forget about clumsy artifices such as *s/he* and *(wo)man*. Some of the following devices may not work in a particular context; we may not succeed in completely uprooting *he* as a generic pronoun, but we can shrivel its roots.

We have at least eight good methods for eliminating sexist pronouns. First, cut the pronoun.

Not this:	*But this:*
The judge should try to read trial briefs as they are submitted to *him* by the parties.	The judge should try to read trial briefs as they are submitted by the parties.
No one may be elected chair after he has reached the age of 75.	No one may be elected chair after reaching the age of 75.

Second, repeat the noun if the repetition doesn't create a clunker. Sometimes, as in the second example below, repeating the noun clarifies the sentence.

Not this:	*But this:*
The judge in whose court the case is first filed has priority in hearing the case. If venue appears to be improper, *he* should grant a motion to transfer venue.	The judge in whose court the case is first filed has priority in hearing the case. If venue appears to be improper, the judge should grant a motion to transfer venue.
If the bailment is gratuitous, for the benefit of the bailor, the bailee is held to only a slight degree of diligence; if the bailment is one for mutual benefit, *he* must use ordinary diligence.	If the bailment is gratuitous, for the benefit of the bailor, the bailee is held to only a slight degree of diligence; if the bailment is one for mutual benefit, the bailee must use ordinary diligence.

But beware: when overused, this method of repeating nouns (*the judge . . . the judge . . . the judge*) gives prose an un-English appearance and tires the reader. Third, make the antecedent plural. This tactic makes the singular *he* unnecessary.

Not this:

A judge should conscientiously meet his responsibility to avoid even the appearance of impropriety.

In the law of illegal gambling, a person who has anything to do with managing the game or table is a principal, whether or not he takes part in the game.

But this:

Judges should conscientiously meet their responsibility to avoid even the appearance of impropriety.

In the law of illegal gambling, all who have anything to do with managing the game or table are principals, whether or not they take part in the game.

Note the possible change in connotation. In the first of those examples, the responsibility appears to be less an individual than a collective one. In the second example, one would be hard-pressed to argue that there could be any real change in meaning. Fourth, use an article instead of a pronoun.

Not this:

Every judgment creditor may use legal means to enforce his judgment.

Nor is it a continuing trespass if a person digs a pit on his neighbor's land and then fails to fill it up.

But this:

Every judgment creditor may use legal means to enforce a judgment.

Nor is it a continuing trespass if a person digs a pit on a neighbor's land and then fails to fill it up.

Fifth, use *who.*

Not this:

Law professors often assume that if a writer cannot write standard English, *he* cannot be expected to understand and analyze complex legal problems.

But this:

Law professors often assume that a writer *who* cannot write standard English cannot be expected to understand and analyze complex legal problems.

The principal has created an appearance; *he* should be judged on the basis of that appearance.	A principal *who* has created an appearance should be judged on the basis of that appearance.
When a person is careless in managing a boat, steam engine, or other machine, *he* will be liable for resulting injuries.	A person *who* is careless in managing a boat, steam engine, or other machine will be liable for resulting injuries.

Sixth, use the imperative or the second person. Although this method has limited utility in legal writing, teachers and commentators may occasionally use it. It assumes a great deal of knowledge about one's readership:

Not this:	*But this:*
The litigator must always take the greatest care when *he* is choosing a jury.	Take the greatest care in choosing a jury. [This imperative statement assumes that the audience consists of litigators.]
When the expert witness testifies not merely to what *he* has happened to see or hear incidentally in a day's doings, but also to *his* expert opinion based on perhaps a lifetime of study or experience in a special career, *he* may demand in advance a special fee proportional to *his* usual professional charges.	If you testify as an expert witness not merely to what you have happened to see or hear incidentally in a day's doings, but also to your expert opinion based on perhaps a lifetime of study or experience in a special career, you may demand in advance a special fee proportional to your usual professional charges. [This statement assumes an audience of potential expert witnesses.]

Seventh, use *he or she* occasionally—not at every turn, but every once in a while, when there's no better method available:

Not this:	*But this:*
A person cannot be convicted of an attempt to receive stolen goods when *he* intended to receive goods while believing they were stolen, but in fact were not stolen.	A person cannot be convicted of an attempt to receive stolen goods simply because *he or she* intended to receive goods while believing they were stolen, if in fact they were not stolen.
The principal should be liable for fraud only where *he* can be treated as being personally responsible for the agent's misrepresentations.	The principal should be liable for fraud only where *he or she* can be treated as being personally responsible for the agent's misrepresentations.

Finally, reword the sentence entirely.

Not this:	*But this:*
A trial judge who decides not to recuse *himself* may continue hearing the case unless an appellate court reverses *his* decision and orders recusal.	A trial judge who denies a motion to recuse may continue hearing the case unless an appellate court reverses the decision and orders recusal.
Whether an offeror has bound *himself* by an obligation, and whether *he* has gotten one in return, is for the law to decide.	Whether an offeror has become bound by an obligation, and has gotten one in return, is for the law to decide.

The English language is steadily moving toward a solution to the age-old pronoun problem in English: like it or not, *they* is becoming a word of indeterminate number. It can be plural here (*they were*) and singular there (*everyone found their way*). Some bemoan this development. But it's now inevitable: the genius of the language is finally solving a problem that has plagued it for centuries. Yet this choice may not be safe now for legal writers: some readers will find you less credible for making it.

As suggested earlier, the generic *he* is not our only problem. We also have suffixes that many perceive to be sexist, as in *chairman, foreman, workman, venireman, testatrix,* and *executrix.* These difficulties can usually be avoided (preferably not by making *-person* a suffix): *chair, presiding juror* instead of *foreman, worker, veniremember,* and *testator* and *executor* (used of both sexes). We may never be able to pry out the sexism from every corner of the language (*manhunt* may last), but with a little sensitivity and effort we can obviate most sexist references without becoming manic.

7.16 Forgo commenting on your words.

Whenever you step out of character to whisper to the reader, you disrupt the flow of the play. Disruptions of this kind usually occur in one of two ways.

First, writers sometimes take out their words to look at them— for example, apologizing for words that need no apology or that should never have been used. We often see this type of distracting self-consciousness (*in a manner of speaking, if you will, so to say, no pun intended*).

> This book does not deal with the institutions of Roman law. It is rather an attempt to describe the political, intellectual, and—*if the expression be permitted*—mechanical forces which were responsible for the growth of Roman law and for its lasting impact on our civilization.[22]

> *Although it is a cliché to say so,* [the book] is in every way encyclopaedic: every form of every description in connection with any Queen's Bench action is here.[23]

> *If the court may be pardoned a bad pun,* National Can is seeking to put new wine into old bottles.[24]

Second, some seek to distinguish themselves from the crowd by showing that they believe their choice of words is much better

---

22. HANS J. WOLFF, ROMAN LAW v (1951).
23. Charles Joseph, Book Review, 83 LAW SOC. GAZETTE 3667, 3667 (1986).
24. National Can Corp. v. Whittaker Corp., 505 F. Supp. 147, 150 (N.D. Ill. 1981).

than that of workaday writers. Quotation marks are the chief abettor:

> After discussion by the board members and comment (or "input," to use the current vogue word) from the public the ordinance was adopted . . . .[25]

It is one thing to shun vogue words (see 2.15); it is quite another to interrupt the message to proclaim that one has successfully shunned one.

Other methods of self-congratulation are possible, and just as deplorable. H.W. Fowler quotes the first example; the second is from a reported judicial opinion:

> They propose to use their powers to force a dissolution. That contingency has been adumbrated (*to revive a word that has been rather neglected of late*); but this is one more case in which we must be content to wait and see.[26]

> [T]he bank may and should be held liable for gratuitously, officiously, and affirmatively—*a surfeit of adverbs never hurt anyone*—telling the government how to place its grasp upon its customer's funds.[27]

Displaying idiosyncrasies—much less drawing attention to them—is unbecoming in the legal writer.

7.17 Ban omnibus words.

Whatever is generic in writing is an enemy to good legal writing. Just as glib generalities weaken the arguments they would support, so omnibus words detract from the message they are to convey. To

25. Condit v. Solvang Mun. Improvement Dist., 194 Cal. Rptr. 683, 684 (Ct. App. 1983).
26. H.W. FOWLER, A DICTIONARY OF MODERN ENGLISH USAGE 733 (1926; repr. 1950) (slightly reworded).
27. Schuster v. Banco de Iberoamerica, S.A., 476 So. 2d 253, 255 (Fla. Dist. Ct. App. 1985) (Schwartz, J., dissenting).

be avoided on this count are highly abstract words such as *area, aspect, case* (when referring to other than a law case), *factor* and *consideration* (in nonlegal senses), *field, important, kind, meaningful, parameters, phase, type.* Expunge these words from your working vocabulary and you will find your writing more vigorous, concrete, and vivid.

Not this:	*But this:*
There are a number of areas in which we might achieve meaningful reform in the field of tort law.	We might advantageously reform tort law in several ways.
The Court failed to provide meaningful parameters for controversial speech.	The Court did not impose express limitations on controversial speech.
An important factor is that we must take into consideration the expense of trial costs in the decision-making process related to a settlement offer.	In considering any settlement offer, we must think about what our trial costs would be.

7.18   Use one word for one notion.

"Besides arabic script, we all learn in school a . . . reluctance to repeat even a single word more than once in a paragraph."[28] Thus, a modern textbook on law for artisans says:

> Except for this potential problem, the *craftmaker's* estate is taxed only on the *craftworker's* share of the corporation. The estate and the beneficiaries receive the *craftsperson's* stock with a fair market value basis . . . .[29]

Just how many people have died here?

---

28. Burlington Indus., Inc. v. Dayco Corp., 849 F.2d 1418, 1421 (Fed. Cir. 1988).
29. L.D. DuBoff, The Law (in Plain English) for Craftspeople 71 (1984) (emphasis added).

H.W. Fowler termed "elegant variation" the ludicrous practice of never using the same word twice in the same sentence.[30] When Fowler named this vice of language more than 75 years ago, *elegant* carried pejorative connotations of precious overrefinement. Today, on the whole, the word has positive connotations. The vice is now more appropriately called *inelegant variation.*

The rule for undue repetition of words is that you should not repeat a word in the same sentence if it can be felicitously avoided. But this rule is hardly an absolute prohibition. The problem is that if you use terms that vary slightly in form, the reader is likely to deduce that you intend the two forms to convey different senses. For example, writers who use *insidious* here and *invidious* there—or *presumptive* in one paragraph, *presumptuous* in the next—almost certainly intend to distinguish the two. We intuitively understand that similar-looking words with different forms have different meanings.

So you shouldn't write *punitive damages, punitory damages,* and *punishment damages* all in the same opinion or brief, lest the reader infer that you intend a distinction. Yet judges have done that, apparently fearful of using the same phrase twice in an opinion, or in a single sentence, as here:

> The law with respect to *punitive damages* is that in order to justify the infliction [read *imposition?*] of *punitory damages* [read *punitive damages*] for the commission of a tort, the act complained of must have been done wantonly or maliciously.[31]

Note how much better the sentence may be rewritten in 14 words instead of 35:

> Punitive damages may be imposed only when the tortious conduct was wanton or malicious.

---

30. *See* H.W. FOWLER, A DICTIONARY OF MODERN ENGLISH USAGE 130–33 (1926).
31. Stenson v. Laclede Gas Co., 553 S.W.2d 309, 315 (Mo. Ct. App. 1977) (emphasis added).

Finally, don't use two or more unrelated phrases to describe a single thing. We confuse readers by writing *leased property* in one paragraph, *demised premises* in the next, and *realty subject to lease* in the next. To a much greater extent than general style, legal style limits a single meaning to the single phrase. If this constraint hinders your stylistic impulses, then rest assured that they're unsound ones.

7.19 Ferret out ambiguities.

Jacques Barzun, the historian and usage critic, once worked with John Simon when the latter was just beginning his career as a film and theater critic. Simon recalls:

> Barzun gave me a number of invaluable pointers about writing, the most astonishing of which was the suggestion that I refrain from using in the same passage the words *regiment* and *calvary* because, in that context, readers were sure to misread the latter as *cavalry*. This struck me as a bit farfetched at the time; still, I dutifully changed *calvary* to *golgotha*.[32]

Retrospectively expressing his gratitude, Simon explains the lesson: "That one could use such foresight and courtesy to forestall misreading—to make some hypothetical reader's sailing a little smoother—is something that would never have occurred to me. Now it is something I can never forget."[33]

Forestall misreading. One common type of misdirection occurs when readers stress a word other than the one the writer intends to emphasize. Take this sentence:

> The average law review writer is peculiarly able to say nothing with an air of great importance.[34]

---

32. JOHN SIMON, PARADIGMS LOST: REFLECTIONS ON LITERACY AND ITS DECLINE 55–56 (1980).
33. *Id.* at 58.
34. Fred Rodell, *Goodbye to Law Reviews—Revisited*, 48 VA. L. REV. 279, 280 (1962).

Is it that the writer can't say anything with an air of great importance? Or that the writer can say something without substance and make it sound very important? The latter, one realizes upon a moment's reflection. But why make the reader think about which of two meanings was intended? A comma after *nothing* remedies the ambiguity.

The self-critical writer rules out phrases such as *dormant sodomy laws*,[35] *alimentary canal smuggling*,[36] and *prophylactics against a wrongful discharge*,[37] which evoke images far different from those intended. Once thrown off track by such a phrase, readers are likely to consider the writer oafish.

To avoid these pitfalls, review your writing ungenerously, as a harsh critic might. If you approach your own writing mercilessly, your readers are sure to be merciful. That brings us to the final point.

7.20 Revise, revise, revise.

"There is no such thing as good writing," Justice Louis Brandeis once said. "There is only good rewriting."[38] Brandeis—who often reworked his opinions 15 or 20 times—would have deplored the "dictator's style" of the modern lawyer—the unfortunate result of "writing" orally into dictating equipment and neglecting revision.

Editing requires different skills from writing. As an editor, even of your own work, you become a critic, distancing yourself from what you've written. The two processes might be analogized to those of the hypothetical–deductive method used in science: the scientist must call upon creativity in posing a hypothesis, then upon critical analysis to test its truth. Both elements are essential.

---

35. *See* J. Drew Page, *Cruel and Unusual Punishment and Sodomy Statutes*, 56 U. Chi. L. Rev. 367, 370, 390 (1989).
36. United States v. Montoya de Hernandez, 473 U.S. 531, 533 (1985).
37. Findeisen v. North East Indep. Sch. Dist., 749 F.2d 234, 238 (5th Cir. 1984).
38. George W. Pierce, *The Legal Profession*, 30 The Torch 5, 8 (1957) (quoting an oral remark by Justice Brandeis).

In revising, the greatest skill is knowing what to reject. Search for every superfluous syllable. If a word or phrase doesn't add to the sentence, blot it out. Every word, every phrase, every sentence ought to have some definable purpose.

At the final stage of revision, read your prose aloud for content and style. You'll be surprised how often you spot subtle problems in the reasoning, or deficiencies in the analysis, by reading aloud. By relying on your ear for guidance—not just your mind's ear—you will also find more ways to improve your phrasing. If you cannot read a sentence or paragraph aloud and have it make sense to a listener, then the writing is inadequate. Work it over again.

Never leave your proofreading entirely to others, or to a computer. Of course, you should ask others to read for you (whenever you can) and use the computer's spelling checker (always). But proofread for yourself as well. Even something as trivial as a typographical error can detract from the message. Perhaps lawyers don't feel justified in billing clients at high hourly rates merely to correct spelling; perhaps some judges consider the task beneath them. But professionalism demands that you take these pains. Finding only misspellings will be rare—more likely, even in the fifth or sixth read-through, you'll find some way of making a substantive improvement. If you find nothing to improve, you'll gain the peace of mind that comes from thoroughgoing care. But it's more probable that you haven't read closely enough.

EIGHT

A Parting Word

A lawyer without history or literature is a mechanic,
a mere working mason; if he possesses some knowledge of these,
he may venture to call himself an architect.

Sir Walter Scott[1]

Writing is an art form. However far we may take the notion of
"legal science," we cannot escape the art of prose, cannot reduce
our use of words to a formula. Rules are helpful because they cod-
ify our predecessors' wisdom. But slavish adherence to the rules is
little better than complete ignorance of them. Merely obeying
rules will never yield literary excellence. That, ultimately, depends
on judgment, intelligence, maturity, and learning—each of which
you ought to cultivate with all the effort you can muster. These
qualities enhanced, your ends as a legal writer become more readily attainable.

Even seasoned lawyers do well to recall Felix Frankfurter's words
to 12-year-old M. Paul Claussen Jr. in 1954: "The best way to prepare for the law is to come to the study of law as a well-read person. Thus alone can one acquire the capacity to use the English

---

1. GUY MANNERING 259 (1815; repr. 1964).

language on paper and in speech and with the habits of clear thinking which only a truly liberal education can give."[2] Law, like literature, is a way of life. If we know and appreciate law, we can understand our society more keenly than before. If we know and appreciate literature, we understand life more keenly than before. Successfully combining the two passions is one of the highest ideals to which a lawyer can aspire.

---

2. Felix Frankfurter, *Advice to a Young Man Interested in Going into Law*, in THE LANGUAGE OF THE LAW 357, 357 (Louis Blom-Cooper ed., 1965).

Eighty Classic Statements About Style

A. Style and Character
B. Style and Content
C. Style as Invisible
D. Style as Clear Thinking and Plain Talk
E. Good and Bad Style
F. Some Additional Precepts of Style
G. The Importance of Style

A. STYLE AND CHARACTER

1. "Height of style is the echo of a great personality."

> Longinus, *On the Sublime* (1st century A.D.)
> (as quoted in F.L. Lucas, Style 49 (1955))

2. "When we see a natural style, we are astonished and delighted; for we expected to see an author, and we find a man."

> Blaise Pascal, *Pensées* (ca. 1655) § 1,
> in 30 *Great Books of the Western World* 171, 176
> (W.F. Trotter trans., 1952; repr. 1993)

3. "Style is the man himself."

> Georges Louis Leclerc Buffon (1707–1788)
> (as quoted in G.W. Turner, *Stylistics* 23 (1973))

4. "The style of an author should be the image of his mind; but the choice and command of language is the fruit of exercise."

> Edward Gibbon, *Memoirs of My Life* 158 (1827; repr. 1990)

5. "Style is the physiognomy of the mind, and a safer index to character than the face."

> Arthur Schopenhauer, "On Style" (1851),
> in *The Art of the Writer* 219, 219 (Lane Cooper ed., rev. ed. 1952)

6. "The writer does not merely give us what he thinks or knows; he gives us himself."

> John Burroughs, "Style and the Man" (1902),
> in *A Reader for Writers* 213, 215 (William Targ ed., 1951)

7. "Essentially style resembles good manners. It comes of endeavouring to understand others, of thinking for them rather than yourself—of thinking, that is, with the heart as well as the head."

> Sir Arthur Quiller-Couch, *On the Art of Writing* 291 (1916)

8. "[J]ust as you cannot make your personality interesting by trying to be original, so you cannot make your style, which is an expression of your personality, interesting by trying to emphasize it or beautiful by trying to adorn it."

> C.E.M. Joad, *The Bookmark* 93 (1926)

9. "To write perfect prose is neither more nor less difficult than to lead a perfect life—indeed the Latins were not far out when they

said that the one cannot be achieved without the other, that the good orator must be, in every sense of the word, a good man."

Walter Raleigh, *On Writing and Writers* 13
(George Gordon ed., 1926)

10. "[I]f you wish your writing to seem good, your character must seem at least partly so. And since in the long run deception is likely to be found out, your character had better not only seem good, but be it."

F.L. Lucas, *Style* 48 (1955)

11. "The fundamental thing . . . is not technique, useful though that may be; if a writer's personality repels, it will not avail him to eschew split infinitives, to master the difference between 'that' and 'which,' to have Fowler's *Modern English Usage* by heart. Soul is more than syntax. If your readers dislike you, they will dislike what you say. Indeed, such is human nature [that], unless they like you, they will mostly deny you even justice."

F.L. Lucas, *Style* 49 (1955)

12. "Good writing is not the perfectly tailored garment of a Personage, perfectly pressed since last he wrote it; it is the rumpled suit of a living person, still relaxing from the strain of his labors, its pockets stuffed with trash and with things worth getting at. And each thing gets its value from the finder."

Martin Joos, *The Five Clocks* 49 (1961)

13. "A really good style comes only when a man has become as good as he can be. Style is character."

Norman Mailer, in *Writers at Work* 266
(George Plimpton ed., 3d series, 1968)

14. "Every writer, by the way he uses language, reveals something of his spirit, his habits, his capacities, his bias. . . . No writer long remains incognito."

William Strunk Jr. & E.B. White, *The Elements of Style*
66–67 (3d ed. 1979)

15. "As Aristotle pointed out long ago, most people do not have the patience or intelligence to follow a logical argument very closely. Most people will be persuaded neither by reason nor by emotion, but by the ethos—the character—of the author."

James C. Raymond, *Writing (Is an Unnatural Act)* 60 (1980)

16. "[W]hat I find most appealing in a writer is an authentic manner. I like to see him or her come across as a vital, companionable human being, not a stuffed shirt or emotionally unfeeling. I like an author to talk to me, unbend me, speak right out to me. If the prose has a natural, conversational rhythm to it, if it's forged out of homespun English rather than highbrow English, if it's stamped with the mark of a quirky personality, if it carries the ring of honesty and passionate conviction, then the writer has captured my attention."

John R. Trimble, *Writing with Style* 65 (2d ed. 2000)

B.   STYLE AND CONTENT

17. "In all speech, words and sense are as the body and soul."

Ben Jonson (1572–1637)
(as quoted in G.H. Vallins, *The Best English* 28 (1960))

18. "Style is the dress of thoughts; and let them be ever so just, if your style is homely, coarse, and vulgar, they will appear to as much disadvantage, and be as ill received, as your person, though ever so well proportioned, would if dressed in rags, dirt, and tatters."

Lord Chesterfield, *Letters Written by Lord Chesterfield to His Son*
350 (24 Nov. 1749) (Charles Stokes Carey ed., n.d.)

19. "Nearly always the things a writer says are less striking than the way he puts them; for people in general have much the same ideas about the matters that form the stock in trade of all. It is the expression, the style, that makes all the difference."

> Voltaire, "Style" (1771), in *The Art of the Writer*
> 156, 160 (Lane Cooper ed., rev. ed. 1952)

20. "The first rule . . . for a good style is that the author should have something to say . . . ."

> Arthur Schopenhauer, "On Style" (1851), in *The Art of the Writer*
> 156, 160 (Lane Cooper ed., rev. ed. 1952)

21. "Have something to say and say it as clearly as you can. That is the only secret of style."

> Matthew Arnold (1822–1888)
> (as quoted in Sir Ernest Gowers,
> *The Complete Plain Words* 12 (1954))

22. "It is only for purposes of study and discipline that we regard style as separable from thought. It is not, and cannot be, something added from without. . . . For ideally style is the thought, freed from crudeness and incompleteness, and presented in its intrinsic power and beauty."

> John F. Genung, *The Working Principles of Rhetoric* 19 (1902)

23. "In the best work the style is found and hidden in the matter."

> John Burroughs, "Style and the Man" (1902),
> in *A Reader for Writers* 213, 214 (William Targ ed., 1951)

24. "Style transforms quartz into an Egyptian pebble. We are apt to think of style as something external, that can be put on, something in and of itself. But it is not; it is the inmost texture of the substance."

> John Burroughs, "Style and the Man" (1902),
> in *A Reader for Writers* 213, 214 (William Targ ed., 1951)

25. "Effectiveness of assertion is the Alpha and Omega of style. He who has nothing to assert has no style and can have none: he who has something to assert will go as far in power of style as its momentousness and his conviction will carry him."

George Bernard Shaw, "Epistle Dedicatory,"
Man and Superman (1903),
in 3 *Bernard Shaw: Complete Plays with Prefaces* 485, 514 (1963)

26. "Most young people, and not a few past middle life, are ever anxious about the style of their speech or composition. Fondly they pore over the writings of some favorite author and wish they might express themselves as gracefully as the language of the printed page. If it could only be remembered that ideas came before words, it might aid in the vexed question of literary art."

Clarence S. Darrow, "Literary Style,"
1 *To-morrow* 25, 25 (Jan. 1905)

27. "Style cannot be distinguished from matter. When a writer conceives an idea he conceives it in a form of words. That form of words constitutes his style, and it is absolutely governed by the idea."

Arnold Bennett, *Literary Taste: How to Form It* 44 (n.d. [1925])

28. "You cannot have good matter with bad style. . . . [F]aults and excellences of style are faults and excellences of matter itself."

Arnold Bennett, *Literary Taste: How to Form It* 49 (n.d. [1925])

29. "Language is to thought what clothes are to the body, and hence should never detract from that which it is intended to adorn."

Frank H. Callan, *Excellence in English* x (1925)

30. "The first of these convictions [about good writing] is that one must have something to say before he can say it, that subject

matter outranks expression, that cargo is more important than ship."

Alfred M. Hitchcock, *Bread Loaf Talks on Teaching Composition* 4 (1927)

31. "To know what you would say and to say it with freedom and with individuality is the great point."

R.D. Blackman, *Composition and Style* 21 (1931)

32. "Matter and manner—we cannot escape them. When they are at one, when what is said has a perfect correspondence with the way of saying it, we have good writing (or speech) on any level. But when this law of appropriateness is broken, writing (or speech) becomes in varying degrees bad."

G.H. Vallins, *The Best English* 199 (1960)

33. "It would be hard to find any reputable literary critic today who would care to be caught defending *as an idea* the old antithesis of style versus content. On this issue a pious consensus prevails. Everyone is quick to avow that style and content are indissoluble, that the strongly individual style of each important writer is an organic aspect of his work and never something merely 'decorative.'"

Susan Sontag, "On Style," in *Against Interpretation and Other Essays* 15, 15 (1966)

34. "The most important principle is so simple as to be almost incomprehensible: *Make sure you have something to say before you write it down.* One of the most difficult things undergrads have to learn is that they have as yet little to say. It's a valuable and humbling discovery, but once a student learns it's almost impossible for him to write anything pointless."

Martin Russ, *Showdown Semester: Advice from a Writing Professor* 25 (1980)

35. "Good ideas are overrated. It makes more difference how a writer handles an idea than what the idea was in the first place."

Andy Rooney, *And More by Andy Rooney* x (1982)

C. STYLE AS INVISIBLE

36. "The greatest merit of style is, of course, to make the words absolutely disappear into the thought."

Nathaniel Hawthorne (1804–1864)
(as quoted in Sherwin B. Nuland, "The Uncertain Art,"
Am. Scholar, Winter 2001, at 129, 130)

37. "The words in prose ought to express the intended meaning, and no more; if they attract attention to themselves, it is, in general, a fault. In the very best style, as Southey's, you read page after page, understanding the author perfectly, without taking notice of the medium of communication;—it is as if he had been speaking to you the whole while."

2 Samuel Taylor Coleridge, *Specimens of Table-Talk* 214 (1835)

38. "[T]he great success in writing is to get language out of the way and to put your mind directly to the reader's, so that there be no veil of words between you. If the reader is preoccupied with your words, if they court his attention or cloud his vision, to that extent is the communication imperfect."

John Burroughs, "Style and the Man" (1902),
in *A Reader for Writers* 213, 226–27 (William Targ ed., 1951)

39. "The law of attention requires that *all writing should reach the comprehension of the reader in the easiest way and with instant clearness.* Writing may be likened to a window through which the writer shows the reader a view without. If the glass is poor it will distort the view and irritate the beholder. Glass made ornate with jewels will draw to itself a part of the attention, and thus impair in-

terest in the view. The best window-glass is plate, a strong and highly finished product so clear that one looking through it is unconscious of its presence; but only artisans of superior skill from long and painstaking practice can produce it."

W.C. Morrow, *The Logic of Punctuation* 14 (1926)

40. "The highest success in a speech, a letter, a sermon, is a demonstration that no attention is arrested by the words or the literary art. The merest touch of quaintness, affectation, eccentricity, literary pretence, cuts off sympathy. The social sense is extraordinarily sensitive to this."

Walter Raleigh, *On Writing and Writers* 20
(George Gordon ed., 1926)

41. "Those who by too great an effort after originality of manner fix attention on their style instead of on their subject have fallen into one of the commonest errors of the present day."

R.D. Blackman, *Composition and Style* 21 (1931)

42. "In everything that concerns writing, I prefer the low tone, no emphasis, no italics, as few exclamations as possible, understatement, irony and humour as unobtrusive as may be. I like a style that never calls attention to itself. No goods in the shop window. A light that is hid under a bushel. As much dynamite as possible, but packed in a box labelled 'harmless.' As much 'rapture' as may be, but under a sober coat."

Van Wyck Brooks,
Opinions of Oliver Allston 287 (1941)

43. "[O]ne can write nothing readable unless one constantly struggles to efface one's own personality. Good prose is like a window pane."

George Orwell, "Why I Write" (1946),
in *A Collection of Essays* 309, 316 (1946)

44. "Prose . . . should be heard and not seen; when the reader begins to see too clearly what made it work, it is no longer working."
James Sutherland, *On English Prose* 28 (1957)

45. "Style is . . . the almost aesthetic excellence of an economy of means to ends, a maximum of effort from an apparently minimal expenditure of energy."
F.W. Bateson, *The Scholar–Critic* 78–79 (1972)

46. "My own belief is that no writing, by anybody, begins to get good until he gets shed of tricks, devices, and formulae."
E.B. White, *Letters of E.B. White* 514
(Dorothy Lobrano Guth ed., 1976)

47. "I do everything in my power to make my writing not look like writing."
Elmore Leonard (as quoted in David Geherin,
Elmore Leonard 96 (1989))

D. STYLE AS CLEAR THINKING
AND PLAIN TALK

48. "He that will write well in any tongue, must follow this counsel of Aristotle, to speak as the common people do, to think as wise men do; and so should every man understand him, and the judgment of wise men allow him."
Roger Ascham (1515–1568) (as quoted in Sir Ernest Gowers,
The Complete Plain Words 261 (1954))

49. "We ought to restrict ourselves, so far as possible, to the simple and natural, and not to magnify that which is little, or belittle that which is great."
Blaise Pascal, *Pensées* § 1 (ca. 1655),
in 30 *Great Books of the Western World*, 171, 174
(W.F. Trotter trans., 1952; repr. 1993)

50. "Style is the disentangling of thoughts or ideas reciprocally involved in each other."

> Thomas De Quincey (1785–1859),
> *Posthumous Works* 225 (Alexander H. Japp ed., 1891)

51. "[N]o style is good that is not fit to be spoken or read aloud with effect."

> William Hazlitt, "On the Conversation of Authors" (1820),
> in *A Reader for Writers* 275, 302 (William Targ ed., 1951)

52. "If you could write lucidly, simply, euphoniously and yet with liveliness you would write perfectly . . . ."

> W. Somerset Maugham, *The Summing Up* 41 (1938)

53. "One should write in the manner of one's period. The language is alive and constantly changing; to try to write like the authors of a distant past can only give rise to artificiality. I should not hesitate to use the common phrases of the day, knowing that their vogue was ephemeral, or slang, though aware that in ten years it might be incomprehensible, if they gave vividness and actuality. If the style has a classical form it can support the discreet use of phraseology that has only a local and temporary aptness. I would sooner a writer were vulgar than mincing; for life is vulgar, and it is life he seeks."

> W. Somerset Maugham, *The Summing Up* 43 (1938)

54. "Generally, style becomes perfect as it becomes natural—that is, colloquial."

> A.R. Orage (ca. 1945) (as quoted in Rudolf Flesch,
> *The Art of Readable Writing* 210 (1949))

55. "Get clear in your mind what you want to say; then say it in plain words and well-ordered sentences. First master the art of simple and clear statement; the graces of style will come later."

> M. Alderton Pink, *Craftsmanship in Writing* 86 (1960)

56. "Good writing . . . comes only from clear thinking, set down in simple and natural speech, and *afterwards* revised in accordance with good usage."

David Lambuth et al., *The Golden Book on Writing* 4 (1964)

57. "Spontaneity, naturalness, a fidelity of the final expression to the original conception—these are clearly intellectual virtues, however we may define them, of supreme value wherever they are found. Overelaboration, whether it takes the form of too many or too few words, is the complementary defect."

F.W. Bateson, *Essays in Critical Dissent* 189 (1972)

58. "Try to get your speaking voice in your writing. You would never say, 'This radio needed repair from the date of purchase'; you would say, 'This radio hasn't worked since I bought it.' In talking, you tend to use short sentences, plain words, active voice, and specific details. You don't worry about beginning a sentence with 'and' or 'but.' You don't use words like 'shall' or 'secondly' or 'societal.' You would never say 'My reasons were the following' or 'Quiet was the night.'"

Daniel McDonald, *The Language of Argument* 238 (5th ed. 1986)

E.   GOOD AND BAD STYLE

59. "Proper words in proper places make the true definition of style."

Jonathan Swift, "Letter to a Young Clergyman Lately Entered into Holy Orders" (1720) (as quoted in Sir Ernest Gowers, *The Complete Plain Words* 162 (1954))

60. "[E]very ear can and does judge, more or less, of style . . . ."

Lord Chesterfield, *Letters Written by Lord Chesterfield to His Son* 351 (24 Nov. 1749) (Charles Stokes Carey ed., n.d.)

61. "The first beauty of stile . . . is propriety, without which all ornament is puerile and superfluous."

> William Kenrick, *A Rhetorical Grammar*
> *of the English Language* 29 (1784)

62. "Learned men, strong and subtle thinkers, and scholars of wide
and critical acquaintance with literature, are often unable to acquire
even an acceptably good, not to say an admirable, style . . . ."

> Richard Grant White, *Words and Their Uses,*
> *Past and Present* 64 (1870)

63. "Nothing else is so important to good style as good judgment,
for this must determine, after all, every nicety within its scope."

> Ralcy Husted Bell, *The Changing Values*
> *of English Speech* 147 (1909)

64. "We talk of good and bad. Everything, indeed, is good which is
conceived with honesty and executed with communicative ardour."

> Robert Louis Stevenson, "A Note on Realism" (1883),
> in *Learning to Write* 21, 30 (1920)

65. "Carefully examined, a good—an interesting—style will be
found to consist in a constant succession of tiny, unobservable
surprises."

> Ford Madox Ford, *Joseph Conrad:*
> *A Personal Remembrance* 197 (1924)

66. "[M]odern writing at its worst does not consist in picking out
words for the sake of their meaning and inventing images in order
to make the meaning clearer. It consists in gumming together long
strips of words which have already been set in order by someone
else, and making the results presentable by sheer humbug . . . ."

> George Orwell, "Politics and the English Language" (1946),
> in 4 *The Collected Essays, Journalism, and Letters*
> *of George Orwell* 127, 134 (Sonia Orwell & Ian Angus eds., 1968)

67. "Literary good form is whatever keeps the reader feeling at home."

Martin Joos, *The Five Clocks* 67 (1961)

68. "[T]he beauty in organized language is not so much the result of putting beautiful words together as it is putting words together beautifully—into Eliot's 'complete consort dancing together.' It is irrelevant to ask whether the words so organized are beautiful when taken singly. The gestalt formula, that the whole is greater than the sum of its parts, is the right one here. The beauty of a pattern of words is ecological, the property of words in a pattern, not of a sum of beautiful verbal moments."

John P. Sisk, "Sound and Sense of Words,"
in *The Ways of Language* 5, 6 (Raymond J. Pflug ed., 1967)

69. "[A]n inferior style seems to produce an inferior vision—a cheaper or at least a less valuable perception of reality; and . . . a superior style seems to produce a superior or at least a more interesting perception of reality."

J. Mitchell Morse, "Prose Style and the Fall of the Empire,"
Am. Scholar, Winter 1978–1979, at 65, 69

70. "Few people realize how badly they write. Nobody has shown them how much excess or murkiness has crept into their style and how it obstructs what they are trying to say. If you give me an eight-page article and I tell you to cut it to four pages, you'll howl and say it can't be done. Then you'll go home and do it, and it will be much better. After that comes the hard part: cutting it to three."

William Zinsser, *On Writing Well* 18 (6th ed. 1998)

F.   SOME ADDITIONAL PRECEPTS OF STYLE

71. "The two capital secrets in the art of prose composition are these: 1st, The philosophy of transition and connection, or the art by which one step in an evolution of thought is made to arise out

of another: all fluent and effective composition depends on the connectors;—2ndly, The way in which sentences are made to modify each other; for the most powerful ideas in written eloquence arise out of this reverberation, as it were, from each other in a rapid succession of sentences; and, because some limitation is necessary to length and complexity of sentences, in order to make this interdependency felt."

2 Thomas De Quincey (1785–1859), *De Quincey's Writings* 65
(David Masson ed., 1889–1890)

72. "There are some simple maxims . . . which I think might be commended to writers of expository prose. First: never use a long word if a short one will do. Second: if you want to make a statement with a great many qualifications, put some of the qualifications in separate sentences. Third: do not let the beginning of your sentence lead the readers to an expectation which is contradicted by the end."

Bertrand Russell, "How I Write,"
in *The Basic Writings of Bertrand Russell* 63, 65
(Robert E. Egner & Lester E. Denonn eds., 1961)

73. "Nothing comes from nothing. Quality writing is done by people of quality. Robert Pirsig, in *Zen and the Art of Motorcycle Maintenance*, says quality depends on three things: self-reliance, integrity, and gumption. If you are self-reliant, you will not blame your boss, or your mother, or your journalism teacher for the kind of writing you do. Second, you have to like who you are and what you do. If you feel good about what you write, it will show. Third, no matter how many prizes you have won or how much criticism you have received, you have to have the gumption to give it your best, one more time. When Frank Lloyd Wright was 76, someone asked him what his best-designed building was. Without hesitation he replied, 'My next one.'"

George Kennedy et al., *The Writing Book* 133 (1984)

74. "If you work for an institution, whatever your job, whatever your level, be yourself when you write. You will stand out as a real person among the robots . . . ."
                William Zinsser, *On Writing Well* 186 (5th ed. 1994)

75. "[T]he secret of good writing is to strip every sentence to its cleanest components. Every word that serves no function, every long word that could be a short word, every adverb that carries the same meaning that's already in the verb, every passive construction that leaves the reader unsure of who is doing what—these are the thousand and one adulterants that weaken the strength of a sentence."
                William Zinsser, *On Writing Well* 7–8 (6th ed. 1998)

G. THE IMPORTANCE OF STYLE

76. "Style has two separate functions: first, to brighten the *intelligibility* of a subject which is obscure to understanding; secondly, to regenerate the normal *power* and impressiveness of a subject which has become dormant to sensibilities."
        10 Thomas De Quincey (1785–1859), *De Quincey's Writings* 260
                (David Masson ed., 1889–1890)

77. "There is . . . only one merit worth considering in a man of letters—that he should write well; and only one damning fault—that he should write ill."
    Robert Louis Stevenson, "Miscellaneous Observations" (ca. 1882),
                in *Learning to Write* 78, 82 (1920)

78. "The most ponderous learning on any subject and the most conscientious efforts to convey instruction cannot succeed without some graces of style. The art of being brief; of touching heavy subjects with a light hand; and of sparing all superfluous detail does not come by nature to all those who have something to say

which is well worth writing, but till this art is gained the best efforts of the beginner must prove failures."

R.D. Blackman, *Composition and Style* 20 (1931)

79. "Style is a magic wand; everything it touches turns to gold."

Logan Pearsall Smith, *All Trivia* 170 (1945)

80. "[A]ny serious writer would do well to think quite a lot about
style."

F.L. Lucas, *Style* 272 (1955)